Deep Down

T·H·I·N·G·S

...Generations have trod, have trod, have trod;
And all is seared with trade; bleared, smeared with toil;
And wears man's smudge and shares man's smell: the soil
Is bare now, nor can foot feel, being shod.

And for all this, nature is never spent;
There lives the dearest freshness deep down things....

—Gerard Manley Hopkins (1844-1889)

Deep Down T·H·I·N·G·S

Poems of the Inland Pacific Northwest

**Edited by
RON McFARLAND
FRANZ SCHNEIDER
and KORNEL SKOVAJSA**

**WASHINGTON STATE UNIVERSITY PRESS
PULLMAN, WASHINGTON**

Washington State University Press, Pullman, Washington 99164-5910
Copyright 1990 by the Board of Regents of Washington State University
All Rights Reserved

Printed and bound in the United States of America

00 99 98 97 96 95 94 93 92 91   1 2 3 4 5 6 7 8 9 10

Library of Congress Cataloging-in-Publication Data

Deep down things: poems of the inland Pacific Northwest/edited by Ron McFarland, Franz Schneider, Kornel Skovajsa.
p. cm.
Includes bibliographical references.
ISBN 0-87422-081-5.—ISBN 0-87422-078-5 (pbk.)

1. American poetry—Northwest, Pacific. 2. Northwest, Pacific—Poetry.
I. McFarland, Ronald E. II. Schneider, Franz, 1928-
III. Skovajsa, Kornel, 1937-
PS570.D44   1990
811'.54080979—dc20   90-24601 CIP

This book is printed on pH neutral, acid-free paper.

Table of Contents

Preface xiii

Acknowledgements.. xvii

Introduction xxi

Floyce Alexander 1
   Poem to Save My Country
   Recuerdo Del Tiempo Perdido
   Red Deer
   The Death of Bertrand Russell

Sherman Alexie 6
   Indian Boys Dream of Icarus
   Poem
   Sinners in the Hands of God

Chris Anderson 9
   Hoko River Project
   Three Stages of the Body

Keith Aubrey 12
   Birds on a Pond at Dusk
   Whalesong

Dick Bakken 15
   Hymn
   Wedding Gift: Four Spoons, a Jar of Honey, Dried Rosehips

Jim Bodeen 20
   Little by Little
   Replenishing the Neighborhood
   Sorting the Spears, the Lead Woman:

Jim Bradford 23
   On a Bus in Eastern Washington
   Two Winter Walks
   For My Father

Randall Brock 27
   Death
   hard
   Poem
   Poem
   the double-quick

Irv Broughton 30
    Pigeons
    The American Dreams
    The Marsh Poets
    Summer's Last Day

Bernadette Carlson 33
    Drops and Bubbles
    Idiosyncrasy
    One
    Wild Meadow

Kent Chadwick.. 36
    Cardboard against the Rain
    For Tom Robbins

Sharon Clark-Burland 39
    Framework
    Postpartum

Gillian Conoley 41
    Rush Hour
    The Cousin at the Funeral
    The Sound I Make Leaving
    Woman Speaking Inside Film Noir

Gary Cooper.. 44
    Come with Me
    Crossing the Sound
    In His Summer
    I-90, Still Heading West

Tom Davis 46
    A Great Day by God
    Being Dangerous Alaska Style
      For a Spokane Native
    The Columnar Basalt of Moses Coulee

Madeline De Frees 48
    Driving Home
    Extended Outlook
    Keeping Up with the Signs
    Nights of Flint and Snow
    Pendant Watch
    The Register
    Tumbleweed

Anita Endrezze 54
    One Thing, Too Much
    The Language of Fossils (Vantage, Wa.)
    The Medicine Woman's Daughter:
      A Charm to Keep You Part of the Whole
    Ways to See

Tina Foriyes 58
    Idaho Vaudeville
    Run-Off
    Sadie's Elegy
    When in Drought

Joan Fox 62
    Fugitive

Philip Garrison 65
    Frames
    from the Fantods

Lynne Haley Slaughter 69
    Conconully
    Geothermal
    Nespelem, Colville Reservation

Mark Halperin 71
    Early October with Cows
    A Song of the Autumn
    Logger on the Upper Klickitat
    The Deaths on Hayward Hill
    Travels

Wes Hanson 75
    Judgment
    Listening

James R. Hepworth 77
    A Short History of Idaho
    Autumn in Inchelium
    Sketches: Colville Indian Reservation, 1975

Christopher Howell 80
    Exclusivity
    Like Feelings
    Poem Based on a Chinese Character Meaning, "A Fire to
      Notify Heaven"
    The Toad Prince
    The Physics of Oh

Marc Hudson 85
    Okanogan Sleep
    Summer, Aeneas Valley
    Voices Overheard on a Night of the Perseid Shower
    Winter, Aeneas Valley

Christiane Jacox Kyle 88
    Oracle
    Six Poetry Anthologies in the High School Library
    Sunday Afternoon
    The Second Language

Eric Johnson 92
    Games
    Poem for a Friend
    Someday
    Thorns

William Johnson 94
    Digging Spuds
    Ode to Steelhead
    Palouse
    Passage
    Vanishing Point

Michael J. Kiefel 97
    By the Sunshine You Ride
    Every Shape that Carves a Color
    Huckleberry Pilgrimage to Mount Thomas

Linda Kittell 100
    Bats
    Island Geography
    Old Home Day

Carolyn Kizer 103
    A Poet's Household
    By the Riverside
    Persephone Pauses
    Singing Aloud
    The Great Blue Heron
    The Worms

Judith Kleck 111
    Crows
    Impromptu for Sarn
    Turning Stones
    Widower

Alex Kuo 114
    A Chinaman's Chance
    A Rose by any Other Name
    from The Picture
    Sheltering the Same Needs
    The River

Laurie J. Lamon 119
    Returning
    Second Lives
    Situs

Eleanor Limmer 122
    Celebration of a Storm
    Liberty
    Spokane Falls in Springtime

James J. McAuley 125
    Drought
    Letter to Richard Hugo from Drumcliff
    Pool at the Y
    Running in Snow
    Spokane Perspective
    The Exile, *En Famille*

Ron Mc Farland 131
    Connecting Flights
    Idaho Chain Saw Massacre
    Man's Death Mars Race
    The Worley Club Cafe
    Why You Think You're in Idaho

James McKean 136
    Bull Slaughter
    Solstice
    Stump Farm
    The Desert
    There's a Hawk in the Yard

James R. McLeod 142
    Archetypes
    Drowning with Brock
    Making the Arrows
    Saying Goodbye

Fran Polek 146
    Similkameen Poems

Joseph Powell 149
    Dreaming Parsley, Winter Soup
    Leveling Grain
    On Finding a Homestead

Steven Reames 154
    Ghosts
    Three Women

Franz Schneider 157
    Little Spokane River: Indian Paintings
    Mt. Stuart: North Ridge in October
    Priest Lake in August
    Travelling East I-90 in the Fall

Molly See 161
    Burned Out
    Daylight Saving
    Sleeping Over
    Summer School
    When It All Comes Together

John P. Sisk 165
    An Aviary
    Sea Prospect: Georgetown
    Sea Prospect: Palm Beach
    The Inadvertence of Being

Ruth Slonim 169
    Countables and Unaccountables
    Cosmic Grammar
    Desert Flowers

Gerald E. Tiffany 171
    Birthday Card to One's Self
    In the Effigy, in the Serpent's Eye
    Water Passage

Patrick Todd 175
    Country Wedding
    For the Memory of Albert Mueller
    Handout at Jacoy's
    Michael Gripping Satan's Hair
    Waking in a Train Yard

Georgia Toppe 181
    Following the Clearwater
    Three Poems for an Autumn Birthday

Mary Ann Waters 186
    Fishing the Jocko
    Glasses
    Seeking the Elements
    Travelling Highway 97: Biggs Junction to Weed

Ronald Webster 192
    At Saint Paul's Jesuit Mission
    Mount Spokane
    William Stafford's Question

Mildred Weston 195
    Aunt Margaret
    Biography
    Birthplace
    Dust Storm
    Landscape

John Neal Williams 198
    Border Crossing
    Sparks

Fay Wright 199
    Like Salt, We are Holy
    The Reading
    The Shape of the Day

Robert Wrigley 202
    Appalonea
    Camping
    His Father's Whistle
    The Skull of a Snowshoe Hare

Afterward 207

Biographies 211

Preface

Travel is one of the great pleasures in life: it stretches the mind, gladdens the heart and enlarges the spirit. That is why millions take trips every year. We enjoy the verve and feeling of vitality that comes from journeys into other landscapes and cultures. Not infrequently, such journeys lead us into the past—which would be impossible if it were not for the many artists and writers who provide us with the images of a place or era. So we often travel far to seek out what they have left behind.

However, such journeys do not always take us to the great capitals or urban centers of a given civilization. As many good travelers know from experience: the true record is sometimes written in the provinces and what endures over the ages is frequently the product of what some would call regional art.

We in the Northwest are no exception. Many fine writers labor here with artistic integrity to give shape and form to human experience in this region. They celebrate its beauty and its promise, but they also make us aware of some realities that could mean the destruction of the good life. They are our voice as beneficiaries of those who came before us and they are our conscience as makers of history for future generations.

The anthology, *Deep Down Things,* makes some of their work available to those who are interested in the cultural and economic well-being of our region. The volume features 56 poets most of whom have been published previously and some of whom have a national or international reputation. All have cooperated enthusiastically in this venture and joined the editors in the hope to place a copy of this book in every city, county and high school library of the Inland Northwest.

We think this anthology does the region proud and is a fitting memorial to the centennials of the states of Idaho and Washington. May it make us more aware of our common destiny and help us preserve our precious heritage as we go forward on the road toward a second centennial.

Special thanks are due to a number of individuals who provided institutional support, practical aid and steady encouragement: C. Michael Archer, Spokane Chamber of Commerce; Dr. Fred Bohm, Washington State University Press; Dr. Michael Herzog, Chairperson, English Department, Gonzaga University; the Honorable Vicki McNeill, Mayor of Spokane; and the Rev. Kevin Waters, S. J., Dean of Arts and Sciences, Gonzaga University.

Most of all, our gratitude goes to the following foundations, individuals and organizations whose financial contributions made this anthology possible:

Dean Robert Brown
Central Washington University, Ellensburg, Washington
President Bernard Coughlin
Gonzaga University, Spokane, Washington
Bud Cox
Spokane, Washington
Eastern Washington State Historical Society
Spokane, Washington
English Department
Gonzaga University, Spokane, Washington
Catherine Gellhorn
Spokane, Washington
Betty Herres-Miller
Yakima, Washington
Johnston-Hanson Foundation
Spokane, Washington
Mathematics Department
Gonzaga University, Spokane, Washington
Norine and Rojer McRea
Aberdeen, Washington
John Michaels
Spokane, Washington
Dean Hugh Nichols
Lewis Clark State College, Lewiston, Idaho
Richard Orfalea
Los Angeles, California
Dean John Pierce
Washington State University, Pullman, Washington
Dean Kent Richards
Central Washington University, Ellensburg, Washington
Seattle Arts Trust
Seattle, Washington
Frank See
Leavenworth, Washington
Spokane Arts Commission
Spokane, Washington

Spokane Inland Northwest Community Foundation
 Spokane, Washington:
  Cosgrove Fund
  Fosseen Fund
  North Idaho Fund

Temporal Acuity Products
 Bellevue, Washington

Mildred Weston
 Spokane, Washington

William Wiley
 Battelle Pacific Northwest Laboratories, Richland, Washington

 Last but not least, the editors express their indebtedness to Dr. Ann Schneider for her many hours of word processing and her astute editorial advice.

Franz Schneider
Gonzaga University
1990

Acknowledgments

Grateful acknowledgment is made to the poets for their generous permission to reprint previously published poems.

Floyce Alexander: "Poem to Save My Country" and "The Death of Bertrand Russell" reprinted from *Bottom Falling Out Of The Dream*, Lynx House Press, Amherst, 1976; "Red Deer" and "Recuerdo del Tiempo Perdido" ("6. Pullman") reprinted from *Red Deer*, L'Epervier Press, Seattle, 1982.

Sherman Alexie: "Indian Boys Dream of Icarus," "Poem" and "Sinners in the Hands of God" reprinted from *Journal of Ethnic Studies*, Summer 1988.

Chris Anderson: "Hoko River Project" reprinted from *Poetry Seattle*, Fall 1980; "Three Stages of the Body" reprinted from *The Greensboro Review*, Winter 1986-1987.

Keith Aubrey: "Whalesong" reprinted from *The Archer*, Summer 1984; "Birds on a Pond at Dusk" reprinted from *The Hollins Critic*, June 1985.

Dick Bakken: "Wedding Gift: Four Spoons, a Jar of Honey, Dried Rosehips" reprinted from *Colorado State Review*, VII, Number 1, Fall 1979; "Hymn" reprinted from *Puerto Del Sol*, Volume 23, Number 2, 1988.

Jim Bradford: "For My Father" reprinted from *New Mexico Quarterly*, Winter/Spring 1969.

Randall Brock: "Poem" reprinted from *Davidson Miscellany*, Volume 6, Number 1, 1971; "Poem" reprinted from *Fragments*, Number 6, 1973; "Death" reprinted from *The Fault*, IX, 1976; "hard," reprinted from *After the End*, Number 4, 1986.

Bernadette Carlson: "Drops and Bubbles" and "Wild Meadow" reprinted from *Changing the Landscape*, University Press, Spokane, 1983; "One" and "Idiosyncrasy" reprinted from *University of Portland Review*, Fall 1984.

Kent Chadwick: "Cardboard Against the Rain" reprinted from *Sojourners*, Volume 12, Number 1, 1983.

Gillian Conoley: "Rush Hour," "The Cousin at the Funeral," "The Sound I Make Leaving" and "Woman Speaking Inside Film Noir" reprinted from *Some Gangster Pain*, Carnegie Mellon University Press, Pittsburg, 1987.

Gary Cooper: "In His Summer" reprinted from *Horizons: The South Dakota Writers' Anthology*, Lame Johnny Press, Hermosa, 1983; "Crossing the Sound" reprinted from *The Green Bowl Review*, 1988.

Tom Davis: "Being Dangerous Alaska Style For A Spokane Native" reprinted from *Wire Harp*, Spring 1986.

Madeline DeFrees: "Tumbleweed" reprinted from *From the Darkroom*, by Sister Mary Gilbert (former name of Madeline DeFrees), Bobbs-Merrill, New York, 1964; "Driving Home" and "Pendant Watch" reprinted from *When Sky Lets Go*, George Braziller, New York, 1978; "Extended Outlook," "Keeping Up With the Signs," "Nights of Flint and Snow," and "The Register" reprinted from *Magpie on the Gallows*, Copper Canyon Press, Port Townsend, 1982.

Anita Endrezze: "The Language of Fossils (Vantage, Wa.)" reprinted from *Harper and Rowe's Anthology of 20th Century Native American Poets*, New York, 1988.

Tina Foriyes, "Idaho Vaudeville" reprinted from *Eight Idaho Poets*, University of Idaho Press, Moscow, 1979; "When in Drought" reprinted from *Idaho's Poetry: A Centennial Anthology*, University of Idaho Press, Moscow, 1988.

Philip Garrison: "Frames" and "from The Fantods" ("2. Adelita from Spokane," "4. Copenhagen Tins") reprinted from *Away Awhile*, Lynx House Press, Amherst, 1987.

Lynne Haley Slaughter: "Nespelem, Colville Reservation" reprinted from *Crab Creek Review*, Summer 1985; "Geothermal" reprinted from *Trestle Creek Review*, Number 3, 1984-1985.

Mark Halperin: "A Song of Autumn," "Logger on the Upper Klickitat" and "The Deaths on Hayward Hill" reprinted from *Backroads*, University of Pittsburgh Press, Pittsburgh, 1976; "Early October with Cows" and "Travels" reprinted from *Seattle Review*, Spring 1987.

Wes Hanson: Quoted material in "Listening" reprinted from *One Day at Teton Marsh*, by Sally Carrighar, Ballantine Books, New York, 1972.

James R. Hepworth: "Sketches: Colville Indian Reservation, 1975" reprinted from *New America: A Review*, 1976; "Autumn in Inchelium" reprinted from *Silence as a Method of Birth Control*, Slackwater Review, Lewiston, 1977; "A Short History of Idaho" reprinted from *Idaho Heritage Magazine*, 1978.

Christopher Howell: "Exclusivity" reprinted from *Mississippi Review*, Volume 17, Number 3, 1988; "Poem Based on a Chinese Character Meaning 'A Fire to Notify Heaven'" reprinted from *Willow Springs*, Spring 1990.

Marc Hudson: "Okanogan Sleep," "Summer, Aeneas Valley," "Voices Overheard on a Night of the Perseid Shower" and "Winter, Aeneas Valley" reprinted from *Afterlight*, by Marc Hudson (Amherst: University of Massachusetts Press, 1983), copyright (c) 1983 by The University of Massachusetts Press.

Christiane Jacox Kyle: "Sunday Afternoon" reprinted from *Southern Poetry Review*, Fall 1979; "Oracle" and "Six Poetry Anthologies in the High School Library" reprinted from *Willow Springs*, Spring 1981; "The Second Language" reprinted from *The Malahat Review*, February 1984.

William Johnson: "Passage" reprinted from *Idaho English Journal,* Spring 1988; "Palouse" reprinted from *Palouse Journal,* Spring 1989.

Michael J. Kiefel: "By the Sunshine You Ride," reprinted from *Reflection,* Spring 1983.

Carolyn Kizer: "A Poet's Household," "By the Riverside," "Singing Aloud" and "The Worms" reprinted from *Midnight Was My Cry,* Doubleday and Co., Inc., New York, 1971; "Persephone Pauses" and "The Great Blue Heron" reprinted from *Mermaids in the Basement,* Copper Canyon Press, Port Townsend, 1984.

Judith Kleck: "Turning Stones" reprinted from *Hawaii Review,* Number 18, 1986; "Impromptu for Sarn" reprinted from *Hubbub,* Fall 1987; "Crows" reprinted from *Ellensburg Anthology,* Four Winds, Ellensburg, 1988.

Alex Kuo: "A Rose By Any Other Name" reprinted from *Northwest Review,* XXII/3, 1984; "Sheltering the Same Needs" and "from The Picture" reprinted from *Changing the River,* Reed and Cannon, Oakland, 1986; "A Chinaman's Chance" reprinted from *Journal of Ethnic Studies,* Winter 1987; "The River" reprinted from *Seattle Review,* Summer 1988.

James J. McAuley: "Drought," "Letter to Richard Hugo from Drumcliff" and "The Exile, En Famille" reprinted from *Recital,* Dolmen Press, Dublin, 1982; "Pool at the Y," "Running in Snow" and "Spokane Perspective" reprinted from *Coming and Going: New and Selected Poems,* University of Arkansas Press, 1989.

Ron McFarland: "Why You Think You're in Idaho" reprinted from *Idaho Arts Journal,* March 1987; "The Worley Club Cafe" reprinted from *Hayden's Ferry Review,* Spring 1988.

James McKean: "Bull Slaughter," "Solstice," "Stump Farm" and "The Desert" from *Headlong,* University of Utah Press, Salt Lake City, 1988; "There's a Hawk in the Yard" reprinted from *Seneca Review,* Volume 18, Number 1, 1988.

James R. McLeod: "Drowning With Brock" and "Making the Arrows" reprinted from *Trestle Creek Review,* Winter 1982-1983.

Joseph Powell: "Dreaming Parsley, Winter Soup" reprinted from *Sundog,* Volume 4, Number 1, 1982; "On Finding a Homestead" reprinted from *The Seattle Times,* March 2, 1986; "Leveling Grain" reprinted from *Panoply,* Volume 4, Number 1, Spring 1987.

Franz Schneider: "Little Spokane River: Indian Paintings" and "Mt. Stuart: North Ridge in October," reprinted from *Roof of Stone,* Temporal Acuity Press, Bellevue, 1982; "Priest Lake in August," reprinted from *Trestle Creek Review,* Winter 1983/1984.

Molly See: "Burned Out," "Daylight Saving," "Sleeping Over," "Summer School" and "When It All Comes Together" reprinted from *Sleeping Over,* Lynx House Press, Amherst, 1979.

Ruth Slonim: "Cosmic Grammar" and "Desert Flowers" reprinted from *Outer Traces/Inner Places,* Three Continents Press, Washington D. C., 1981.

Patrick Todd: "Country Wedding," "Michael Gripping Satan's Hair" and "Waking in a Train Yard" reprinted from *A Fire By the Tracks*, Ohio State University Press, Columbus, 1983.

Georgia Toppe: "Three Poems for an Autumn Birthday" reprinted from *North Dakota Quarterly*, Volume 53, Number 3, 1985.

Mary Ann Waters: "Glasses," "Fishing the Jocko" and "Seeking the Elements" reprinted from *The Exact Place*, Confluence Press, Lewiston, 1987; "Travelling Highway 97: Biggs Junction to Weed" reprinted from *Poetry*, CLI, Number 1-2, 1987.

Ronald Webster: "William Stafford's Question" reprinted from *Alternatives*, The Best Cellar Press, University of Nebraska, Lincoln, 1987.

Mildred Weston: "Aunt Margaret," "Biography," "Birthplace," "Dust Storm" and "Landscape" reprinted from *The Green Dusk: Selected Poems*, Owl Creek Press, Seattle, 1987.

Fay Wright: "The Reading" reprinted from *Out of Season*, Confluence Press, Lewiston, 1981; "Like Salt, We Are Holy" reprinted from *Willow Springs*, Spring 1984.

Robert Wrigley: "Appalonea" and "The Skull of a Showshoe Hare" reprinted from *Moon in a Mason Jar*, University of Illinois Press, Urbana, 1986; "His Father's Whistle" reprinted from *Northern Lights*, Volume 3, Number 4, 1987; "Camping" reprinted from *Poetry*, June 1988.

INTRODUCTION

All poetry should have a local habitation . . . . We should make poems on the familiar landscapes we love, not the strange and glittering ones we wonder at.

—*William Butler Yeats*

This anthology provides the broadest sampling presently available of contemporary poets of the Inland Northwest: an area roughly circumscribed by the towns of Spokane, Colville, Omak, Wenatchee, Ellensburg, Yakima, Richland, Walla Walla, Lewiston, Clarkston, Pullman, Moscow, Coeur d' Alene, and Sandpoint, as well as towns in the Big Bend country. Apart from our insistence that all selections possess literary merit—and some works here must be judged outstanding in terms of even the most stringent aesthetic considerations—our choice has been shaped by geographical rather than formal or thematic criteria. As part of Washington's and Idaho's centennial celebration, in a time of heightened awareness of our historical and cultural identity, we believe such an anthology will prove useful both for us and the generations to come, for poetry documents as well as illuminates events, experiences, attitudes, and emotions in ways not accessible through other sources or media.

The manner in which the contents of this volume were assembled has at least one direct consequence upon how these poems relate to one another and what they may be expected to reveal when viewed in their entirety.

Between September 1988 and January 1989, we invited the poets of this area to submit three to five pages of work—published as well as current—from which the present selections have been drawn. While we sought as wide a range of subject matter as possible, we did suggest that the poems reflect the life and history of this region. We are deeply grateful to the poets for their generosity. Especially appreciated was their assistance in alerting us to fellow practitioners whom we otherwise might have overlooked. But the salient feature to be noted is that the poems of this anthology are not "typical" or "representative" or "meritorious" as defined by editorial fiat. They were offered by the poets themselves and reveal, albeit indirectly, what the poets consider to be regionally important, what they think deserves to be preserved and remembered. While it would be naive to assume that the poems mirror the character and concerns of the population at large, or even the attitudes and values of the poets themselves, they clearly do represent a spectrum of *poetic* concerns. In a very real sense, collectively these poems constitute a literary self-portrait of the Inland Northwest.

Whether the general reader should be conscientiously attuned to this feature of the poetry is debatable. After all, by their very nature anthologies, like a well-stocked pantry, are designed to appease a diversity of appetites and our cavalier perusal of them is sanctioned by a long and happy tradition. In the classroom we invariably alter sequences or omit sections as students are led to construct alternate conceptual frameworks or pursue different interests. The reader is warmly encouraged to luxuriate in an equal sense of freedom: skim, savor, or skip as habit, inclination, or whimsy may prompt. Revisit the familiar or explore the new, for poetry does not need the support of critical scaffolding. Poems speak for themselves and poetry provides its own justification: here, a scene sketched with laser sharpness; there, a feeling delineated with surgical precision; and always the delightful play of cadences, rhythms, and sounds of varied voices—a rich record of women and men of keen sensibility responding to their world thereby enriching our experience of it.

At first glance, to be sure, the contents of this volume appear to mimic the variety and the breadth associated with the eclectic character of contemporary American poetry in general. But by reflecting more deeply upon this material we may discover more similarities than differences, may discern shared traits, features, and concerns. In short, we may find a degree of homogeneity that justifies thinking of these works as regional art. The following observations touch upon those aspects. They are not offered as a framing perspective that would force others to see these poems from one limited point of view but, rather, as almost a postscript, something to glance at perhaps after having reached some conclusions about this body of poetry. We hope they shall be found useful, but won't be disappointed if by challenging or quarreling with them the reader brings his own views into sharper focus.

II

. . . one's verses should hold, as in a mirror, the colours of one's own climate and scenery . . . .

—*William Butler Yeats*

As a term in art history, "regionalism" refers to certain features associated with a specific locale—its people, customs, and landscape—as found in the fine arts and the literature of various periods. American literature has always been richly infused with a sense of place, but the deliberate exploration and elaboration of the distinctive character of the several regions of the country did not gain full momentum until the last decades of the nineteenth century. Then "local color writing" achieved wide acceptance quickly, and continues to be an abundant element in the present. Its historical origin is the fusion of a Romantic concept with a Realistic method: it places a high value upon individuality, distinctiveness and singularity, and combines that with a dedication to verisimilitude, the wealth of concrete detail that constitutes the tangible nature of physical reality.

Precisely because of its great popular appeal and commercial lucrativeness—not only here but in Latin America, the Commonwealth nations, and Continental Europe as well—the "Regionalist" label is often applied disparagingly to designate works that are narrow, provincial or parochial in conception, and odd, quirkish, peculiar, strange or non-conventional in execution. The critic's pejorative stance is not simply an elitist aesthete's animus toward commercially popular art in general. Rather, it alerts us to the fact that the very source of regional Realism's strength can easily become its limitation, for far too often its success is fueled by audience expectations and demands that have nothing to do with aesthetic value. On the one hand, indigenous patronage of the local fine arts—when not miserly and penurious—tends to be enthusiastically uncritical. In its encouragement and praise it is not unlike fond parents who cherish even an under-exposed, poorly focused, compositionally banal snapshot of their child simply because it is their child, a part of their life and their experience. On the other hand are the outlanders, the curio seekers, the collectors of the exotic, who are infatuated and charmed by anything that contrasts sharply with what they perceive to be their own commonplace, quotidian existence. When combined, these two groups provide an eager market that overwhelms many a local talent constraining it to produce unintentional parodies or burlesques along the lines, for example, of the flood of seascapes mechanically constructed out of popularly conceived de rigueur elements: sand, surf, sky, sail, seagull, sunset.

While literature and especially poetry is less susceptible to such pressure since its "product" is not as clearly marketable as pictorial or plastic works, it is not immune to the laws of the marketplace. But at its best, when the purely local is imbued with universal significance, when the particular comes to stand for the general, when, in Whitman's image, the grass blade supports the universe upon its point, then we have art of genuine scope and power.

None of the poets present here strives to be programmatically regional, but poetry is grounded always in personal experience: a poet responds to the world around him and his response, in turn, bears the imprint of that world. The most obvious of such traces are local place names. Indeed the magic of names is the *sine qua non* feature of regional literature. In the realm of the imagination these small clusters of syllables become powerful conjuring wands capable of producing a variety of effects. They provide more than an instant demarcation of locale. Poets delight in their euphony as well as in their evocative, associative energy—mood, feeling, atmosphere—in a small compass. Names are the accent pigments on a palette of local color and this anthology vibrates with their hues: Inchelium, Worley, Aeneas, Conconully, Nespelem, Klickitat, Wenatchee, Yakima, Okanogan, Vantage, or St. Regis, to list a few. For a conveniently brief example of how effectively such purely local names can be incorporated into a much broader frame of reference we may look at "Down by the Riverside."

In the poem an adult speaker recalls how as a child she lived "by a real stream, Hangman's Creek,/ Named from an old pine, down the hill/ On which three Indians died." Two of them "were thieves/ Strung up by soldiers from Fort Wright in early days,/ But no one remembered who the third one was." In the child's imagination the historical legend lives again attached to a real tree on a hillside which, in turn, comes to be associated with a much older execution site, the hill of Calvary. When later, still as a child, in the same creek, in winter, she sees a "buck-naked" old Indian and his squaw bathing—he, "Breaking the thin ice with his thighs. . . . Proud of his iron flesh, the color of rust"—that experience joins with the other two to form a permanent complex of feelings that outlives the subsequent changes that wholly alter the configuration and character of the neighborhood. Thus a purely topographical and historical feature of Spokane's South Side becomes the locus of archetypal images of "god-head and manhood," symbolic models that appear in various guises in the maturing consciousness of every adolescent. Though we do not live at "1-3-7-5 Riverside" Avenue, our habitations are situated on the banks of the same stream of life from which these eternal experiences emerge.

A less complex but commonly employed method of enlarging the significance of regional material can be illustrated by reference to indigenous occupations. Various types of labor associated with the Inland Northwest are amply represented: ranching, farming, lumbering, mining, trucking, harvesting, cultivating, picking, tilling, plowing, herding, dousing, milling, even teaching—all find their place in these poems and cumulatively provide a firm sense of its people's bond with the land, its resources, and each other. While it would be dangerous to make easy generalizations about attitudes toward labor from these examples—its role and function differs from poem to poem—it seems safe to say that in a large number of instances such labor is felt to be a part of an unbroken continuum of mankind struggling for more than mere sustenance, striving for some measure of freedom from the constraints of earning its daily bread. "Leveling Grain" may serve as an illustration.

Like interstellar distances, or the national debt, the sheer volume of grain produced in the region strains its storage facilities and our comprehension, as anyone who has seen the mountains of wheat dumped on open ground will attest. The Herculean magnitude of the task facing the persona in this poem is clearly indicated in the opening lines: "Imprisoned in a tin silo/ I leveled grain with a scoopshovel." Desiccated, mouth and eyes and skin "coated with blond dust," he finally reaches the apex of the mountain and emerges into the open air. There, "looking out over the fields," he thinks

            of all the years
        the centuries of people
        breathing the grains's dust
        under a hot sun—
        Joseph & the Jews,
        Gentiles and Indians,
        Chinese and Africans,
        the long human chain
        that linked me to them.

The centuries old human chain, of course, is a common poetic device which by superimposing the present upon the past reveals the common features of both. It is interesting to note, however, that here as well as in other poems, the focal emphasis falls upon "the coins or promises/ spilling from their fingers/ like grains of wheat"—that is upon the hoped for and expected rewards of such labor which always elude "them"—rather than upon the wheat itself. The closure of the poem clearly suggests that the dream of escape, or relief from the bondage of labor, is a universal illusion by substituting for the microscopic vision of the laborer a macroscopic view: "seen from an airplane" the speaker "was only a part of the earth/ beside a silver flash of life" reflected from the minuscule grain elevator. Reduced ("leveled") to a speck of insignificant dust, the speaker's dream dissipates in "soundless air." And yet the word "silver" in the penultimate line provides the final flash of insight: there *is* precious wealth here but not in the form expected by those who amass it.

There is another way, perhaps the most interesting way of all, in which indigenous material can evade the charge of mere provincialism. Instead of evoking an archetypal aspect or revealing a universal nature, the poet may choose to emphasize an intractable singularity that forces us to recognize and accept something on its own terms. Foreign and odd though it may be we incorporate it within the pale of our own experience by virtue of the powerful presence it assumes in our imagination, for the character of the region is constituted no less by its imaginative possessions than by social, economic and political ties. The fate of a typical aging town may serve as a convenient example.

The life cycle of dozens of small communities throughout the Inland Northwest exhibits a common and familiar pattern: several decades of rapid growth and expansion followed by generations of slow decay. Eastern urban centers die in their hearts; in the rural West die-off is more likely to occur on the fringes. As a defensive maneuver not only is retrenchment easier sometimes than evacuation, it also is more in keeping with the spirit of pioneering settlement, the reluctance to let go of what has taken so much hardship and sacrifice to acquire. Who for example, has not seen the ubiquitous "empty house/ by the road at the edge of town/ its windows whiskered with lilac/ and letting in rain" ("Palouse"). A compelling development of this theme may be found in "Travelling Highway 97: Biggs Junction to Weed."

This poem is as much a tribute to Richard Hugo, "trucker laureate/ of western towns," as it is a moral portrait of a truck-stop village, since the travelling couple (only one voice speaks for both of them) make a conscious effort to observe and to feel as Hugo might have, had he visited Biggs. On their way to Mexico from Spokane they pass through "Dorris, a sharp left turn of a town/ with everything in collapse/ but a neon toucan above an empty marquee." That toucan, like the abandoned Palouse house, is an emblem, a mute sign of time's dominion, but what greets them is worse, for here "the problem is not decay." In a savagely Juvenalian vein they note that in this "crossroads of convenience" there is no hope, "No history, no dreams. What counts now is asphalt, diesel, gasoline, and cash." The scathing tone that records the schlock reality of the place alters when the speaking persona, as they enter a restaurant, pretends to see Hugo "leaning up against the counter/ by the till." Recalling his dictum "to find something here to love . . . or to forgive," the two of them indulge their own cleverness in a burlesque that proclaims Biggs as "The birthplace of generic":

> the Greatest All-American Generic Town,
> home of the mashed potato, canned tomato soup,
> toasted sandwiches of Velveeta cheese.
> The town bird, the sparrow. The color,
> asphalt-grey so grey it's black.
> The mascot, any mongrel passing through.
> The motto: no shoes, no shirt, no service.
> The obvious regret, no shopping mall.
> It's always Tuesday, 5 p.m. in Biggs.
> It never snows. No one plants a lawn.
> No crime. Prairie dogs come here to die.

The tone shifts again as they retire for the night to the Nu Vu Motor Inn with its "desperate yellow paint." In their room "the pillows are like shelves,/ the single window opens to the parking lot below."

These rich modulations in tone—from caustic to ironic through longingly elegiac to dispassionately objective—firmly establish Biggs Junction as a presence to be reckoned with, a place that unabashedly, unapologetically, and imperiously lays claim to our attention. Coarse, vulgar, offensive, and yet virulently alive, it is a blight, an eye-sore that insolently asserts its right to exist. Like an irritating burr, it clings in the folds of our memory even if we encounter it only in this poem.

III

. . . what is this separate Nature so unnatural?
What is this earth to our affections?

—*Walt Whitman*

In "The Marsh Poets," when a curious tourist inquires what poets do, he is told that "they live off the land." The figurative meaning of the phrase provides an apt umbrella term under which, in a sense, almost every poet in this anthology finds shelter at one time or another. Explicitly or implicitly, immediately or distantly, almost every poem presented here touches upon Nature—a subject so vast one can only sketch in a few of its features. In a classic study, A. O. Lovejoy distinguished at least sixty-six different senses for the terms "nature" and "natural," and yet even such an ample taxonomy seems scarcely adequate to capture all the shadings of the concept and the variety of attitudes it engenders. For our purposes it may be enough to note that these poems reveal an unmistakably neo-romantic sensibility: they are part of a tradition that flows from Wordsworth and Keats through Hopkins, Whitman and Dickinson to Frost, W. C. Williams and Lowell—a lineage whose most proximate mentors for these Inland Northwest poets are Roethke, Hugo and Stafford.

Literary tradition, of course, is not a simple matter of influence or conscious imitation, much less a question of conceptual determinism along lines suggested by biological models. It should be thought of, rather, as a loose and fluid continuum of similarities, parallels, and congruencies shared by members of a community of kindred souls laboring in the same vineyard. Seen in this light, the neo-romantic view—often more a matter of temperament than philosophical conviction—is characterized by a cluster of assumptions, attitudes, and value judgments whose broad features are easily outlined.

In general, it manifests itself in a predisposition to accord honorific status to primary rather than secondary qualities, to the innate and given rather than the acquired or developed aspects of reality. To use a currently fashionable idiom, the romantic believes in Nature and mistrusts Nurture. That logically speaking the two are a function of each other, that they cannot be conceived except in terms of one another, does not trouble many romantics, for theirs is a partisan stance, an allegiance to, and therefore a repudiation of, one or the other side of what is perceived to be an antithetical schema, a polarized notion of man and his relationship to others and the world. In practice it means a preference, in all things, for the "natural" rather than the "artificial," regardless of how these terms are defined; a reliance upon the affective rather than the cognitive faculties as a means of gaining knowledge; a faith in individual intuition and a suspicion of common consensus; an interest in private experience and a disdain for life in the public domain; a cultivation of spontaneity and self-expression rather than socially mannered behavior; and a recourse to the past rather than the present as a touchstone of authenticity—in short, a thorough skepticism of civilization whose blandishments, in the inner ear of the romantic, sound like, to misquote Wallace Stevens, an ill-tuned "blue guitar/ that does not play things as they really are."

But deafness or indifference to the Siren song of society is not a safeguard against other seductive melodies, since the neo-romantic himself becomes helplessly spellbound by primitive pipings, the sounds of Nature's myriad voices. As a cultural phenomenon, it is difficult, at times, not to view the worship of Nature as an urban sentimental fantasy—a current version of pastoral. And yet, to be overly critical of the escapist element of this dream is to miss its therapeutic function. The urbanite's yearning for intimacy, for rapport, for communion with primal life-forces becomes formalized in rituals of healing, of ceremonial cleansing. For many the return to Nature is primarily an attempt to slough off the detritus of city life—its mechanical din, its tedious materialism, its stifling social routines. The shrill demands for increased productivity, efficiency, and profit can be muted temporarily or openly defied by immersion in activities where such qualities become meaningless. Therefore, we should not be surprised to find in the formulaic expression of these longings a quasi-religious fervor, a thirst for spirit that has become Nature. Thus the week-end pilgrimages and mid-week reveries that seek contact with that mysterious presence whose noumenal visage tantalizes the parched sensibilities of those who earn their daily wage in the asphalt desert are but a modern version of what Carlyle called "natural supernaturalism."

Fortunately for us, the dramatic presentation of these notions in the poetry itself is not at all as tediously arid as the above sketch of them might suggest. That is so, first of all, because the history of American poetry in general, and perhaps Northwest poetry in particular, has been profoundly affected by the theory and practice of Imagism whose strong antipathy toward a poetry of ideas was one of its most obvious features; and secondly, because in literature ideas are not the abstract products of cogitation but aspects of character or pattern of action. They are a part of our experience and so intimately bound up with it that to speak of them as ideas at all seems violently unjust, a wrenching apart of something that in our imaginations—and our very nerves and muscles—seems to exist as an indissoluble whole.

Imagism was not a school, a movement, or an "-ism" in the usual sense of these terms. Though they were the contemporaries of the memorably voluble Post Impressionists, the Imagists had no manifesto, no roster of members, and no public programme; and perhaps even their poetry is of less importance than Ezra Pound's (b. Hailey, Idaho) widely broadcast formulation of what he perceived to be their principles. Foremost among them was his insistence that poetry be dramatic, that it deal with its subject—which could be literally anything at all—"directly"; that it "present" instead of "describe" in a condensed, concrete fashion; and that it "Go in fear of abstractions" never retelling "in mediocre verse what has already been done in good prose." Pound's influence, his role as publicist of the "new poetry" can hardly be overstressed, particularly when we also take into account his observations about verse forms, meter, rhythm, and the primacy of "musical phrasing."

When it comes to prosody, more than a few of the poets in this anthology have also heeded his advice to "Read as much of Wordsworth as does not seem too unutterably dull." At their disposal, by now, is a formidable array of techniques which, gratefully, they employ as the occasion demands rather than for their own sake. From one of the strictest of medieval fixed forms, the sestina ("Indian Boys Dream of Icarus"), through the ubiquitous sonnet and blank verse, to free verse scarcely distinguishable from heightened prose, the metrical and melodic effects of the poems in this anthology, for the most part, are functional rather than ornamental. The aural harmony of rhyme, when it makes its infrequent appearance, serves the same function as the harpsichord continuo in Baroque music: it provides a solid substratum against which the foreground of thematic development can display its distinctive character.

Thus in "Cardboard Against the Rain," the irregular, at times elliptical syntax disrupts and modifies the enveloping rhyme scheme. The resultant tension effectively heightens our engagement with the poem's core experience, a struggle for dignity amidst the disorder of poverty. Or in "Six Poetry Anthologies in the High School Library"—which details a teacher's startling discovery of a secret, unsuspected sensibility in one of her dull, boozy, mechanically adept but verbally clumsy students—we are struck by the deft aural lacing of rhyme, particularly in stanzas four to nine, whose pattern the reader discovers, in a manner analogous to the persona's own stunning *post-mortem* revelation, only after examining the poem carefully, a second time around. Or as our last illustration, we may note the evocative power of "The Language of Fossils" which is due in no small part to the complex manner in which the triple sense of language—as sound, as sign, and as object of discourse—is richly elaborated. Not only is the latinate terminology itself a remnant of a dead language, a most satisfying vehicle for an ossified subject, but the very friction of "vowels like flat stones .   .   . and consonants like a bone/ caught in the earth's throat" produce a cacophony of sounds that, like the "calcified waves" themselves, embodies the full sense of "*stillflow*": though dead (as in still-born), yet it flows and it flows still.

The point to be noted here is that—whether prominent, as in the above, or slight and unobtrusive—melody and rhythm make their presence felt. Since they are not an attribute of the thing presented, they unavoidably draw attention to the human dimension, the human control, the human significance of the thing itself. For nothing in a poem is merely a thing, a pure entity in its own right. It is always an object of human interest and acquires its value only in terms of the field of human perception which brings it into focus, details its features, analyzes the function of its parts, and develops a sense of its meaning. No can of snuff is capable of seeing itself as a "metal blossom" in an "arroyo/ flashflood of cans" ("Copenhagen Tins"). The impression of the thing, never the thing itself, is what poetry, and art in general, re-presents.

In addition to formal constraints, concepts in poetry are prevented from taking free flight by being grounded in the psychology of character or persona. Though a number of these poems invite us to reflect on high level abstractions like fate, destiny, chance, the nature of being, purposiveness, design, mutability, permanence and so on, such cerebral matters are inextricably enmeshed in temperaments whose singularity defies all attempts to categorize or generalize them. While most of us have heard of Bertrand Russell, who among us has ever conceived of meeting him in the guise that confronts us in "The Death of Bertrand Russell"? Though we may be more or less familiar with the cult of the Noble Savage, who would envision his Colville Indian counter-image:

> Rousseau! you slobbering imbecile
> the people marry poor
> die poor   bitterness
>
> to beat hell out of the day
> lovers spawn in the shadows
> by the lake race their flashy cars
> up and down the highway
> until the blur of dawn

Nor should we overlook the most troubling puzzle of them all, how the notion of good and evil is "planted deep in our small hearts" ("Michael Gripping Satan's Hair").

And the sheer waste and pointlessness of an innocent child's death—of most deaths for that matter—has left many a thoughtful mind reeling, but take a look at "For the Memory of Albert Mueller" (or, for a strikingly different treatment, "The Great Blue Heron") to see how a poem handles such situations. Or finally, to curb one's tendency to illustrate endlessly given the wealth of what might be construed as cerebral poems, let us glance at "Wedding Gift: Four Spoons, a Jar of Honey, Dried Rosehips" in which "aunt/ Alva,/ five times a bride,/ who drank like a fish, flopped/ with her men, and woke up/ dead in bed alone/ in her mountain cabin." The poem is a meld of feelings that flow through three generations producing a web of conceptual intricacy that a few lines of commentary can never hope to untangle. And yet even a first reading will convince readers that they are in the presence of physical laws that Newton wholly left out of his account as they note that when the sumptuously Rabelaisian "Alva breathed, men/ started alive, apples fell to the ground."

In summary, the intention of the above examples and comments is to demonstrate that while the social and cultural expressions of neo-romantic sensibility are often sentimental, in poetry that sentimentality is transformed if not expunged, by virtue of formal, dramatic, or psychological determinants. Pure emotion or feeling is incommunicable; it does not become intelligible, and thus capable of being felt by others, until it is attached to, or embodied in sound, color, object, or situation. To present it in perceptible form is one of the functions of art. We may close now with the central issue itself: the concept of Nature in these poems.

By and large what most absorbs the poets in this anthology is the natural, tangible world around us. They are fascinated by its unceasing mutability which yet occurs in cycles or in keeping with immutable laws— an organic world constantly perishing, yet everlastingly reborn. The sense of an animate Nature is inescapable: we see here a living land seeded with bones and the "tongues of ancient beasts," alive with memories, breathing, rolling, heaving, swelling, slumbering, waiting, watching or, perhaps, simply being. One thing is clear, it cannot be ignored. Its hills, mountains, and forests; its valleys, plains, and fields; its lakes, rivers, and streams; and its boundless sky by day, wheeling constellations by night, are not merely the setting of life in the Inland Northwest—they are its very texture and substance.

We should not be surprised, therefore, to find numerous word paintings, macro and micro views, prospects, and a propensity for Whitmanesque catalogues of flora and fauna—a full complement of life forms swarming beneath a stellar canopy, a multitudinous company that would have dismayed Noah, an assemblage that only a literary ark can contain.

The manner in which this profusion is brought to our attention is especially gratifying. For the most part it exhibits many Dickinsonian virtues: economy, condensation, sparseness, absence of affectation or self-consciousness, and a sincerity and naturalness that captures the direct impact of sensation on perception (see, for example, "Okanogan Sleep" or "Early October with Cows"). Also in evidence is the legacy of W. C. Williams and Roethke: a clarity and intensity of focus that at times seems almost surreal, particularly in detailing the "twigginess" of plant life, whose monomaniacal energy, hidden for so long in the dark of humus and soil and decaying leaf, suddenly sprouts forth in a sensuous unsheathing of curling tendrils, revealing naked life in all its moist, almost queasy splendor (see "Digging Spuds" and others in a similar vein). This rich presentation of detail is more than simple delight in the inexhaustible riches of corporeal Nature. It is also a way of checking or taming excessive sentimentality, for feelings are not merely painted over the core situation or event, but inhere and arise out of the very details themselves as in "Hymn," "The Deaths on Hayward Hill," or in "Ghosts."

And Nature's character is perhaps most in evidence when we recognize that ultimately no poem is merely a record, a verbal equivalent of something out there. No matter how clinically objective it may appear, it is never mere perception: always and foremost, it is a subjective, inner vision of external reality. No one knows, perhaps no one will ever know, what purpose the world of matter has apart from mankind. But whether we see in it our likeness or whether we view it as something foreign, a life other than our own, in both instances the only significance we can ascribe to it, or pretend to discover in it, is inevitably a function of our involvement with it. And for this reason we value so highly the vision of those poets who, in Coleridge's phrase, possess the "esemplastic" power, the ability to perceive unity in diversity, wholeness in discreteness, traces of an organic life in the spume of inert matter.

Most often this sense is aroused by stressing the grand scale of Nature, what the older Romantics called its "sublime" aspects. The felt presence of the invisible in the visible, of the permanent in the mutable, is generally more accessible when we concentrate on cycles, mystical connections, and grand designs. Such visions may be sacramental or assume largely secular expression as in "Come With Me" where, in modernist fashion, the archetype of fishing is fused with the myth of the Fisher King to evoke the sense of an Eliotian arid wasteland of spirit. But it can also be found in anomalies, those occasions when systems break down or seem to malfunction, as in "Whalesong." Beached on the gently sloping level sands near Florence, Oregon, for three days a pod of sperm whales "sang/ A compline of alien clicks,/ Hums, whistles" until, their "whaleroad . . . ended," their carrion is bulldozed into a bonfire pit, and

> The fires, fed with wood, tires, alumagel,
> Burn softly out. The whales,
> Lifted by thick smoke
> Into the wind, return in rain to the sea.

The image of the smoke (a blend of inorganic, organic, and man-made compounds), which itself is "recycled" by Nature in the form of rain, is a perfect "objective correlative" for the central insight of the poem in which the widening evolutionary gap, the "distance of relation" between creature and man, is bridged by death.

This theme—the interwoven Oneness of All Creation—finds its most compressed expression in "Seeking the Elements," in which earth, air, fire, and water—so central to the Ancient, Renaissance, and Neoclassical mind—become a romantic pentad at that moment when, in some out of the way meadow, with the children waiting in "the Star touring car," the water spoke through the branch and the douser became more than mortal man, not just "anyone's father. For here was the place/ where the willow wanted to become water,/ the water to become sky,/ the douser to become earth,/ the earth to become fire."

But ultimately the most satisfying view of Nature is the one which can be apprehended in a single intense contemplative gaze, one in which the awesome scale of the subject is contained within the compass of a lyric frame that allows us to concentrate on the persona's relationship with the land: the point at which the personal joins the universal. While a number of the poems in this volume focus on this omphalitic seam, in closing let us concentrate on two that display this theme in pure, succinct distillation.

In "Passage to India," Walt Whitman asks, "What is this separate Nature so unnatural? . . . . (unloving earth without a throb to answer ours,/ Cold earth, the place of graves.)" We might almost take "Birthplace" and "Biography" as an answer to that question. The persona of these two poems begins with what is unquestionably the most given aspect of life: "time set the pins that hold me/ here transfixed within my region,/ finding what grace I can/ standing at this place." Although she may have been seeded here by the vagrant winds of chance, when her childhood takes root it establishes a "kinship" with "vine or vein, whatever grasped the earth." Her very being—just as the mixture of "animal, vegetable, mineral" elements in the natural world—is a compound "of soul and body mixed" which, in turn, is amalgamated with the features of the Big Bend plateau whose "dry lands" give "weight and structure,/ tissue to my name." Unlike Shelley's "Ode to the West Wind," the omnipotent wind-spirit that shapes the very contours of the land and its inhabitants is here seen in humanly comprehensible terms:

> Full-circled plains   .   .   .
> place me in bitter grandeur
> to live as the earth turns:
> frozen in darkness, parched in sun
> with horse rider and soil tiller
> who bend to their obdurate master
> the veering wind.

One cannot improve upon the incomparably forthright expression of this sense of oneness with the earth.

Kornel Skovajsa
Gonzaga University
1990

Floyce Alexander

Poem to Save My Country

Now when the long night drags its dress of ice and fire
across my face, I blink and steady my body
against the wind's thrust between my shoulderblades,
conjuring you, country, woman, history
riding between my teeth, a metal bit,
horse saddled with the past, with no future,
looking for the waterhole of dreams, good water.

In Mexico I was embraced by scarred children
in rags, the early damned, selling Chiclets, mothers
begging through swollen lips, blind mariachi
in Patzcuaro by his empty sombrero,
by the greatgrandmother of Lazarus,
and the boy who walked all day on his knees,
screaming Dinero! at the passing tourists.

In Mazatlan I was invited to the shack
of a drunken transit driver on his day off,
Sunday, to share his tortillas and caldo,
and to take his daughter's hymen in his bed,
but when he left the table to get sick
I took my body walking down the beach,
staggering from so many gifts, and back

to America, my own still-life country bleeding
through lacerated eyes, body puffed and bloated,
back to the open veins of the land, the blade
adorned with stars and stripes hanging from the sky,
back to this town of withering women
whose shapes are knolls and sex the thawing snow,
back to corrals where horses stamp all night

to stay warm. States! I should have gone with my gypsy.
You saw her coming and denied her an exit.

You held her long hair in your hands and laughed
when her body tried to run on without her.
America! your face covered with blood
in the boiling sun, bleached dull gray under
the howling moon, washed by the stormy seas—

who is there to stop your plunge into the abyss,
who would dismantle your arsenals and give us
men rather than idiots for high office,
who would give blessing to the dreams of children,
and would bury the heathens John Calvin
and Cotton Mather, set fire to this ice
at least, make a peace we have never known.

Recuerdo Del Tiempo Perdido

6. Pullman
In the hills always cold where deer shod fresh snow
even in summer the Little Sand's currents prickled
your pink skin the crayfish nipped with orange talons.
Two years lived alone, Sartre, Dostoevsky, Karl Marx,
Thoreau in a rowboat among the reeds casting for trout.
Writing letters, mannered poems, narcissistic essays,
getting paid for propaganda. At first cockroaches
swarmed the attic so I drank and slept on my desk.

Married twice. Once and poems broke the old leash.
Twice and one night I wanted to die for a live word
on my lips. On the last day I walked in grass high
as my waist, dry as kindle, and next door the sculptor
visited to tell me my departure was the end of an era.
My friend the hermit came up the hill to help me pack.

Red Deer

I

I was running out of money for gas on the way east,
I discovered on the New York State Thruway,
A little south of the Seneca reservation that holds
All that's left now of the Iroquois.

I thought of debt, of starvation, of dispossession.
I thought of the woman who sent her man to the forest,
Armed and hungry, with the words in his head
That said one after another bring down red deer.

Red deer. Blood to be drunk, flesh to be eaten.
Red deer only quench the thirst, sate the gnawing teeth
In the stomach's maw. Red deer only leap
Into the eye of the hunter's arrow in mid-air.

2

II

I ditched the car near Albany, began to thumb
Past Albany, nearing the border of Massachusetts
Where King Philip was slain in a whorl of blood and dust,
Where none of Narragansett, Pequot, or Wampanoag survive.

I thought of genocide, I thought of plunder without quarter.
I thought of Sir Jeffrey Amherst, of his smallpox-infested
Blankets sent among the people the land was stolen from.
I thought of this, walking into Amherst, crossing the Common.

Red deer. At night they come down from the meadows
Of the moon to graze in the meadows of New England's
Bony guilt-harvested minds asleep under gabled roofs
Of three-story mansions handed down by assassins of red deer.

III

I wake out of deep sleep with the taste of hooves
On my tongue, the smell of the herd on my hands.
Here I know no-one, where everything leans toward
Me and seems to say my name. Red deer, red deer.

I no longer live in my home country, the West.
The West is a garden of space, a river of sky.
I load my home on my back, I leave this island
Of mackerel, of lemming, things too close to death.

I follow the tracks of red deer, follow them West.
I follow the scent of red deer all day, all night,
And sleep out the day between, dreaming of red deer
Crossing the Adirondacks, the Plains, the land between

The grave of the Old East and the garden of the West
Where a human grows; then wake once more, red deer.

IV

I think again of the woman sending her man
Into a forest, hungry and armed with the words
In his head and saying them one after another
By the mountain stream to bring down red deer.

I think again of debt, of starvation, of dispossession,
Of genocide, of plunder without quarter,
Of the land torn from under the hooves of red deer.
I think of the disappearance of my countrymen

The devils killed with their smoke-belching wands,
Ploughing graves just ahead of the falling bodies.
Near the Rockies, the last trek begins. I hear
The herd beyond the reach of fingers in a dream

Climbing, climbing. Here I am alone with red deer,
Descending where my country opens out and into years.

The Death of Bertrand Russell

Yakima Roy Conant, d. 21 February 1970

Near the end something was caught in his chest
Or throat,
So you could hardly hear him tell
For the first time
The story of James J. Jeffries
And how many wives.
It was boxing he loved most
Though his friends might insist later his wife
Was the subject he never forgot,
The only one he had and left
To hop a freight heading for Omaha
Or Liverpool.
Most of those who listened don't remember
Having heard him mention Bertrand Russell.

The first time
I met him he was sitting on a stool
In front of his cabin
On the first day of spring.
The bitch dogs were getting chased by the studs,
And the tomcats were stalking the pussies
Down the driveway.
He had just repaired Miss Latta's lawnmower.
"I used to get around better
And keep the place up
For Alice.
Last few years my bones don't mesh
So good."

I did a lot of drinking and he did
A lot of talking that day.
He told me about Peter Jackson
And the way he finished George Carpentier
Before Bob Fitzsimmons,
And the night Firpo knocked Dempsey
Out of the ring. I mentioned Gene Tunney.
"That man was smart. He read a lot.
Some men read and never fight.
Now take that Limey, what's his name,
Russell, he's in the papers
Saying our boys are doing the same thing
The Germans did in World War Two.
Now don't get me wrong,

I don't see how he's right,
But by God he's a fighter, that's for sure.
I remember one time I had money,
I bought one of his books.
He said a lot of things in it
I didn't and never will understand.
I don't know whose fault it was,
I guess mine.
I don't read much anymore but westerns...
He said in this book that the truth
Is the hunger inside a man
And not just the food he eats."

Sherman Alexie

Indian Boys Dream of Icarus

I acknowledge you, Indian Boys,
dancing alone on the high hills.
Hair threaded with wild ponies,
sky pulled down in your hands,
drums thunder across your chest:
old voices echo in my hollow bones.

Walking past jumps where bones
of buffalo lie buried, I watch boys
gallop across grass, their chests
thin as feather. Climbing hills,
horizon stretched between my hands,
the earth rolling like wild ponies

where the ghosts of roan ponies
graze, I hear the song of bones.
The air opens a mouth and hands,
I hear the voice of Indian Boys;
their fire climbs the high hills,
Icarus descends into their chests.

I hold his head to my chest,
the child that dreamed of ponies
hunted by wolves on dark hills.
He wanted to find their pale bones
and carve flutes for Indian Boys
who grew up afraid of their hands.

I take his heart in my hands
and tear it from his chest.
Using blood to reinvent boys
who run beside the wild ponies,
I pour it from hollow bones
and it flows down the hills,

a river that runs until the hills
are perfect again like hands.
I crush earth in bones
and rub it across their chests.
I paint eyes of wild ponies
onto wild eyes of Indian Boys.

I dream, Indian Boys, alone on hills.
Desire wild ponies loose in my hands,
my narrow chest. We wear the same bones.

Poem

"oh children think about the good times"—Lucille Clifton

we lived in the HUD house
for fifty bucks a month
those were the good times
ANNIE GREEN SPRINGS wine
was a dollar a bottle
my uncles always came over
to eat stew and fry bread
to get drunk in the sweat lodge
to spit and piss in the fire.

no one never had no job
but we could always eat
commodity cheese and beef
and Mom sold her quilts
for fifty bucks each to whites
driving in from Spokane
to buy illegal fireworks.

that was the summer I found
a bag full of real silver dollars
and gave all my uncles all
my brothers and sisters each one
and no one spent any   no one.

Sinners in the Hands of God

she, who once was my sister
dead in the house fire
now lying still in the coffin
her hair cut short
by an undertaker who never knew
she called her hair 'wild ponies'

I don't know any beautiful words
for death or the reason why
sinners curl like blackened leaves
in the hands of God

she, who once was my sister
is now the dust
the soft edge of the earth

Chris Anderson

Hoko River Project

"These Indians of the Hoko River had developed a sophisticated technology for deep-water fishing thousands of years before they encountered the white man."

—Dr. Dale Croes, Director, Hoko River Project

He scratched with a toothbrush
In the clay along the Hoko,
Tagged the fragments by lantern:
Lines, leaders, weights, spreaders,
The bones of halibut and sole
Among the powdery embers. In the fall rain
He dreamed of the Makah hunkering down
By the fire, biting bone onto line,
Stretching knots with both hands.
Scouring shard in a wooden sieve,
He glimpsed the curve of a hook,
Thick, melting into lime, imagined
Kelp line stiffening in dark water,
Jerking against the bark of a gunwale
A thousand years before.

Winter he bent plumwood into hooks,
Tied bone to the hook shank
With split spruce roots, soaked kelp
In saltwater and dried it by the fire,
Fixed it to the pole with a square knot,
To the hook with a clove hitch.

Flat days on gray water.
He kept checking the bait,
Slicing off chunks of squid.
The kicker drifted far beyond
The mouth, the blank line of trees,
Out into the Strait of Juan de Fuca.
Bottom fish spit out the hooks
When he dangled them in the tanks
At the Aquarium. An old Makah
From the village knew enough
To flatten the spreader,
Lengthen the barbs.

9

A sudden storm in spring.
Quickly hauling line into coils,
He didn't feel the drag on the spreader,
The flutter of current, the rising
Of the sole in the waves.
It flapped softly in the bottom
Of the boat, flat and featureless,
The hook shank stuck like a burr
In the gristle of its tiny mouth.

That night he hunkered down by the fire,
Baked the catch in alder coals.
In the journal he wrote:
The Hoko is widening into the strait.
Fog drips in shadows of fir.
Bones hiss in the ashes.

Three Stages of the Body

I

There is a knowledge
Only the hands have
Pressing and clasping.
The feet know something
About the hard ground.
Running, I feel the fact
Of things in my lungs.

Shadows fall away.
I know the weight of my body
Standing in a room.

I am subject to gravity!

II

Blessed be my joints
Rotating and gliding
Like pulleys.
Blessed be my blood
Coursing through
The mysterious circuitry.
Blessed be my myriad systems
Slipping and turning
And meshing precisely.

III

All this time
There was a path
Through the woods

To a waterfall.
There was a castle
On a hill
And the streets
Strewn with banners
And the villagers
Thronging for the festival,
Laughing.

Inside me all these years
Was a great space
Like a cathedral.
I am standing on the edge
Of the cavern marvelling.
My ribs vault up over me
Farther than I can see.

Keith Aubrey

Birds on a Pond at Dusk

Turnbull Wildlife Refuge, May 1984

At the Wildlife Refuge, waterbirds make
Mad chorus: yellowheaded blackbirds,
Those senile emphysematics, laugh
From reeds; coots bicker,
Thrashing the placid water.
Tree swallows burp like babies
While snapping up gnats and mosquitoes.
Canvasbacks skip love calls
Across the pond that mirrors wood and clouds.
Redwinged blackbirds make spastic
Song in the pines. I sweep my hat
Overhead to scatter mosquitoes.

A yellowheaded blackbird
Wheezes, swoops to a reed
With wings spread back, feathers
Fantailed, the cold reptilian
Claws wide open. Chickentailed
Baby grebes thrum like greasy
Evinrude trolling motors
Refusing to start. Canadian honkers
Sound beyond the wood. One
Ponderosa pine outtrunks
The rest, silhouetted at dusk
Like a Japanese silkscreen. The balls
Of my feet tingle, my heels ache;
Tucked in like a child
Under these dark clouds, I close
My eyes. The sweet smell of the pond
Spins me back to summer vacations.
A mosquito whines in my ear and, far
Away, sounds of the highway
Rush, a great horned owl moans.
The north wind rises, bruising
Needles; it rushes through the mossgrown
Ponderosa wood
Hundreds of miles inland
With the surge and fall of the tide.

Reflections dim on the water.
A ghostly heron looms
Overhead, veers toward the sunset
And glides to the horizon.

Night sets over me, leaving
Only the sounds
Of wings on the water.

Whalesong

Florence Beach, Oregon—June 1979

The tide wanes, the mirrored sun recedes.
Slowly dying fires
Flicker the evening with oily smoke.

Five nights ago, flashlight beams
Revealed a beach
Strewn with sperm whales, whose flukes
Clapped the wet sand
Helplessly, under the evening star's
Descent. All night people gathered;
Electric light poured through the pale
Effluvium. A long
Rope was stretched in a jagged
Halfcircle around the beach; a photographer
From a local paper was held
Back by police, another man
Posed with his boy. Hands
Tested, tested the smooth taut skin.

By morning the crowd had swelled; the tide
Returned with lengthening reach. A seabreeze warmed,
Pushing the thick stench inland.
Marine biologists performed crude
Autopsies with knives, syringes,
Chainsaws, as the living whales
Crushed themselves to death with their own weight.
The tide full, a group of people staggered
In the cold surf, dragging
A small whale through deep red sand, until
The rope sliced into the fluke. The whales sang
A compline of alien clicks,
Hums, whistles; rotting
Flesh was scarred with bleached
Rings, brands of giant squid
That gorged themselves on black a mile below.
Over these, orange numbers
Were painted; pink diatoms that still
Clung to their hosts died with them.

The third day, euthanasia. Veterinarians
Injected M-99, rangers drove
Harpoons through ribs to collapse lungs, severed
Arteries that blew blood.
Scrimshawers salvaged teeth;
Others salvaged anything, and carrion putrefied.

This whaleroad is ended. The last day, gulls
Flew and feasted; county workers
Bulldozed a bonfire pit.
What gravitated the whales here? what
Drew the people, here?—only distance . . .
Of waves, of undersea canyons;
And the distance of relation: the spirit's evolution.
Darwin's genealogical lines
Strain up through time, farther
And farther removed from their common source,
To form a canyon only death can bridge.

The fires, fed with wood, tires, alumagel,
Burn softly out. The whales,
Lifted by thick smoke
Into the wind, return in rain to the sea.

Dick Bakken

Hymn

Nigger, my grandfather's dog, a horse of a hound
pulsing with the animal in his own blood. Ray Virtue,
a hard man, a carpenter, a grandfather with hands
large enough to cuff a steer dizzy. He could never
comb his thick hair down. His blood drove him always
to mountains and fast streams. From sunup he walked
the deer trails with more wind than a boy could breathe.
If Grandfather stopped to wait, his eyes got impatient
and wild. He taught me the woods and cuffed me silly
with his hands, for I learned well but was a fool
and never saw quick how a cutthroat must be hooked *so*,
gutted *so*, how a line does not tangle if handled *so*,
how both a man and a dog must care for themselves.

Tired old Italians sold Grandfather a farm and left
their dog. From hayfields around the house the hound
stood watching the wild-haired foreigner clear out
the yard with his large hands, blowing windy oaths,
ripping up grapevines tangled crazy with morning glory.
Supper after supper Grandfather set out venison gristle,
then at cockcrow the dog stepped over new glory vine
to sniff. In time he answered to Nigger, which echoed
like his Italian name Grandfather would not call.

Caring more for his corn than for the blood in a dog,
Mansfield down the road, a windless farmer and bad shot,
one day hit Nigger in the foot and the dog did not come
home till apples fell. Like Grandfather he cared to breathe
his own wind and not limp in front of others. The hound
slipped in behind Grandfather milking and watched his hands,
who finished up before taking Nigger in his carpenter arms
from the barn, to rouse me out and show his foot was nearly
healed, his blood yet inside him, his animal pulsing.

All one dawning, Grandfather walked home after rebuilding
a cabin in the mountains. His farmyard shone in blooming
glory Sunday noon when he puffed in, shaking his great
head of hair. As he whistled over his yard, big Nigger,
from out of nowhere, came galloping and sliding twice
around the white farmhouse kicking up dust and tearing
grass, then leaped ten feet through sunlight to flop
sweaty and dirty in my laughing grandfather's arms, still
shaking all through with the animal in his blood.

Long ago Mansfield down the road shot Nigger in the head
and he could not come home or hold in the blood spilling
out in the corn. Now my children are nearly ready to walk
the woods and Grandfather won't be there to teach them.
But he still has all his wild hair and some of his wind,
and I know he can knock me over with the back of his hand.

O Nigger, as a boy I saw you race twice around the house
and leap ten feet into my grandfather's broad arms!

Wedding Gift: Four Spoons,
a Jar of Honey, Dried Rosehips

You are Sally, Bride, and Aunt.
Sister, you will be Mother.

1
These silver spoons
were a wedding gift from our aunt
Alva,
five times a bride,
who drank like a fish, flopped
with her men, and woke up
dead in bed alone
in her mountain cabin.

In Alva's sheets
I kissed my bride from ears to toes
and breathed all night
faster than the river was sliding
by
while she sighed
Help me.

We woke marvelling
to be groom and bride, flesh
tart with brine,
bodies
dappled new with blood, smelling
of milt and roe.
We slipped together
and did not think to fathom
our dream:

16

Alva, dizzy as a lord,
rolled in her billowing lace
and did not hear
the river rushing away.
She hung on to each thrashing groom
and cried
Sweet, I am dying.

2
You are named Sally for me
after the first
girl I loved, but Pamela
sallied me sweeter and slicker than any—
O quick as a fish I was quivering
and done.

Cockcrow and cockcrow,
hips bright on the briers, I woke
to kiss her shining belly. We rose
to pump and fire
our bath and the tea
and splashed with the sucklings
who made you aunt.

When Alva breathed, men
started alive, apples fell to the ground.
She whirled and maple leaves slid
away on the water.
We loved our bodies rising
from her bed and kept our sap
warm,
stirred honey in tea with these
spoons, now yours.

Drinking while the river went
shallow, under slipping cedar shakes
in our hands
hips fell apart in the teacups,
like the cabin and everything else,
leaving dregs to mull
and dream:

Alva—lord! juiced to the gills!—
raising
her cup to good health.
She tossed off groom after groom
and roared, swigged
her applejack and merry and cockeyed
stumbled to bed too stiff
to get up.

I sat up cold in Alva's sheets
with drafts rolling the curtain lace,
over and over
geese flying the river
away south.
Pamela lay waking in linen
far away as the swells that billowed
by while I unveiled
my bride.

3
All Alva's grooms though they fumble
in her sheets till sap and the river flow
back, fear they will come
to nothing
but the damp and draft.
Sally, I'm chilled stiff
by bride's lace, and curtain, sleet,
slush, ceiling, and bed
in a heap—thickets to bloom,
pheasants awake—
where her hips and Alva's
rose and rose.

The velocity in our blood, heat
in our breasts, fails
to quicken frost from the maples and ice
from the water.
We always ebb and sleep
though newly wed and drunk
as lords.

But a bride and her groom
though they cry help from their bed
do not fail
to come to their death.
A bride though she die and die again
only wakes in the salty air
niece and aunt,
a bride, unlaced, wound in sheets
with her groom.

4
Bubbling Sally Lovelace
made me blush and grin when I was a boy
and you woke up
alive.
Because now
you are aunt and Sally in veils
and the river does not flow
back,

here is honey to your health
and silver spoons. You need only a cup
to fill
and raise and fill
and the dregs to tell what blooms
for a rosy wink.

Here is to Sally dressed up
in a curtain, dreaming the playhouse
bride. Here is my face
shining.

Eric is in my lap, Pamela
seeded with Creseyde.
Here is Alva walking toward us, well
water brimming in her
cup.

And here is today
in the mountains—where the cup
lies still against the cool
pump.

Jim Bodeen

Little by Little

the asparagus
is going away.

It does not want
to be here.

So skinny
with its flower

on top, drooping.
So hot, under

the sun, even
this piece

of poor land
is tired. It

is sad to cut.
Mother calls it,

Weeping penis
of an old man.

The boss needs
to water. We

can't stay
for 40 boxes

and make wage.
All the families
walk sad rows
in sad fields

waving goodby
to asparagus.

Replenishing the Neighborhood

In late May
the young Mexican
comes to the door
in the evening
selling asparagus.

Orchard this morning

He gives the price
and I give him the money
wondering
if these tender spears
came wild
from the side of the road
filled with pesticide
and spray, or from
the cutters in the fields,
and I think of the picture
they ran in the paper:

women strapped, harnessed,
dangling from irrigation pipes
hovering inches from the grass,
an innovation
to save their backs.

Packed in the Del Monte Box,
stalks to the outside,
delicate tips like feathered hands
clasped, true produce
of our labor.

Taking the lug from his trunk
grateful for no common language,
we shake hands, look at the stalks
and smile at the precision
of the mitered cut.

He drives off to his own life
under the safe light
of the evening street
and I carry the asparagus,
this slashing meditation,
to the back porch.

Sorting the Spears, the Lead Woman:

Rich women
use these spears
to stir vodka.

Everybody here knows that.

The best spears go
into vodka, pickles,
or to Japan. What
we do—
make sure
no one complains
when they sit
to drink and eat.

Spears go in 3 sizes.

7,8, & 9 inches.

Short & tender bring
the big money
and fly farthest.

Saws cut to our eyes.
Conveyor belts take the butts
to a truck,
nothing gets thrown.

What we do here is sort.

I'm experienced.

That's why I'm up front.
My cold hands
decide what to keep
and what to throw.

When it leaves me
it better be right.

This warehouse now,
it's not air conditioned for women.
It's for asparagus.

My lead lady, she's gone today.
Son's getting married.
She's my interpreter.
These women sorting.
Mostly single, alone.
What they sort here is asparagus.
They learn fast. It's cold,
and constant.

Jim Bradford

On a Bus in Eastern Washington

1.
The moon
is a sun

flower
in the snow.

2.
There's Spokane!

Nope.

Just moonlight
on the snow.

3.
Winter fog, blind from birth,
more pure,
even, than the snow.

Two Winter Walks

for Debby Jacquemin

ONE: Saturn in Leo

After a snow
the sky clears
and the temperature drops:
I rejoice in the sun,
in my coat and gloves,
in the ice age victory
of the warm blooded animals
over the great reptiles,
and in the existential
affirmation
of my solitary tracks.
Each crystal of snow
holds the image of the sun:
I walk in billions of suns!
I give them voices
and they say:
"I'm the sun!"
"No, I'm the sun!"
Then I imagine the sun
arguing thus
with the other stars,
but I can't imagine
the beginning of light,
the beginning of time.

TWO: Neptune in Capricorn

The second scene
is of gray
and white silence
but for the crunch
of my boots.
I stumble:
the light is flat,
but the surface is not,
although, after awhile,
the snow rises,
and each flake
drifts off
to fill the emptiness
of the universe;
and the earth,
and the sun,
and all the matter
in the universe,
flakes apart
until all that remains,
ever so slightly
above absolute zero,
are protons
faintly glowing
as they disintegrate
and disperse.
And as I wonder
"Into what?"
I try to imagine
the end of space:
it's as if my mind
were two facing mirrors,
and my astral body, a sailor
who falls overboard
and feels the ship recede,
until I find myself,
here and now,
in the center of everything
like everyone else.

For My Father

A man in a white suit
is handsome in the sunlight

Falling behind his eyes
are granite cliffs

Coils of ice
are faster than the eye

Guilt edged pictures
every several frames

White on white

Randall Brock

Death

    the edge
of a forest
as wings
      become silver blades
      hacking my eye.

hard

dark
dead edge
of/a thin
air
in sleep
seizing
yr hand

Poem

lost
days
enduring
until
the
guard
got
caught
training
his
orphans
as a
catch-
can
existence
exploded
& then
believed
that
desire
formed wings
on
tips
of
bent
heat
at
day-
      break.

Poem

tell me
about
your conclusions.
tell
me the
way you
reach
for your
gun.
hold the
pigeon
& take
heed
of death.
let
me see
your horse—
the saddle
that
never fits.
the cow-barn
&
dung
from
that incoherent
squirrel.

i

  fight

     you!

the double-quick

bar
of eternity
floats
in a
     dozen
places
over maps
without names.

Irv Broughton

Pigeons

The fog like quicksand
slows movement.
The pigeons come head-on
to the glass of wind.
Turning sideways on the balusters
in the high, white clouds,
they think of the richness of their blood.

They think of sickness, loneliness
in the highest ridge
of themselves as they follow the updraft
of the gun the janitor uses
on them, soiling the sky.

The messages they carried rise like clouds.

The American Dreams

for Bobby

I dream a Chinese.
He falls,
Newly arrived in America.

I dream crevices
Will keep us
From falling.

I dream of missing
Grandfather
By only three years.

Before me the winds lob
Off clouds
And the mountains

Sacrifice the water
They have gathered
To the flat land.

I read grandfather's
Book, and dream
Those people rubbed together

As you'd turn pages.
He wrote about
Immigration law:

Loosely-bound words
Turn slowly
In that Chinaman's nervous

Hands, butterflies
Filled with dozens
Of Americas.

The Marsh Poets

Fourteen poets
live outside town,
near the marsh
and when the fog
settles,
as it inevitably must,
they busy themselves
designing
mutations of words
coming on like Santa
after the first
full snow.

One
makes windows
for others
to stare
at the blank
bare fog.
Whatever brought them
together,
separates them.

A tourist asked
what did
they do
and was told
they live
off the land.

Summer's Last Day

At the Cape rotary
the bright cars or bus
flares off like light
reflected from a pinwheel,
in the direction of Bourne.
A tourist sign lifts
like a rib in the wind,
and a dog scampers out from
under the noise. I think
of our last swim yesterday,
as we pass a car with a flat
thumping on the road like storm waves.

Bernadette Carlson

Drops and Bubbles

"An upper level disturbance is approaching the Cascades
and will reach Eastern Washington this afternoon."

weather

report

Reflecting on the forecast—
morning exercise on the lower level—
I ask the five-year-old
waiting for his sister's music lesson to end,
if he knows what disturbance means.
He guesses: to bounce up and down on the bed?
I think of the rough road the wind takes
in the trees and clouds and the dusty-fresh
scent of coming rain.

Falling on his hand, a first drop makes him laugh.
I contemplate drops, their complexity;
three-part, some of them, a shell around a shell
around a core, like a double coated seed.
Rising in liquid drops take bubble shape
and burst at the air interface.
We watch the bubbles in the sprinkler puddle,
small popping balloons breaking so fast,
I warn, you can't chase them
like your dandelion seed umbrellas.

A surprise gale sends blossoms flying past,
small butterflies, thick as snowflakes,
to settle on the curb where pine cones bloom.
The two of us run with them under the blue-glass cloud.
Quickly as it rose the wind falls.
The myriad grass and the parched-beak robins
stand up to the hesitant globes, slanting fog pearls.
The wavering curtain impinges, the upper level spills over,
and from the porch we listen to the dry ground drinking.

Idiosyncrasy

I'm not able to read this book
until I find a bookmark.
Dog-ears and any-old-markers dismay me.
My eye falls easily on what will fit,
everything from calling cards
to magazine inserts for fine china,
so they please my taste
and the book deserves them.

Before returning, I flip the pages
and remove my marks but I can be generous,
calling into play the next reader.
I leave them in the volumes I own
to know how to go where I've been,
rediscover a discovery forgotten
where, as in a pomander
savors I want to sift again
wait for me.

One

Dark is its theme
heavy to wake with,
a current of sadness
into the day.
Eyes would flow over gates
and downstream drown,
build distraction from whatever
company, comfort, beauty.
Not blinked or smiled away
when I pray, "Why go I weeping?"
Is it my own—ancestral haunting?
or Gerard's "chief Woe, world-sorrow"?
I wait dark's discerning:
Borders open on streaming peoples,
bowed pain. My shade their shadow.
I would find the way I must walk
or be stranger to all those names
wearing in mirror image a face I know.

Wild Meadow

1

Unlike the dandelion
baroque and signalling light
the buttercup is classic,
narrows design to
focussed form,
art so relevant as
to seem unoriginal.

2

Swirling between
the pine boles
that blue cloud
breaks into rain
of blue bells.

3

The meadow is full of eyes.
Browneye in yellow fringes
in a thousand repetitions
gesticulates *I am.*
Wind from the cliff makes
a brown and gold commotion
and time gathers up
the lovely gesture.
The world I see with second sight
leans me toward home.

4

That improbable zone
opens on the airs and light
of another spring
come once and always.

Kent Chadwick

Cardboard against the Rain

Mama at the door shakes her head slow, she just stare
      Feel the wet wind slap like Cain
      Filling her place cold, where
Children crowding that blank window pane
      Move the tired rug, the lame chair
      Raise cardboard against the rain.

No, she can't hear them ask, instead
      Dangles while antique despair
      Swings her over lives spread,
Smeared open on cardboard; damp, taunted
      Sees her children born then them dead
      Molded in fine final clothes they wanted.

Scared with imagining she can't fight
      Down soft whining dread,
      Taheerah reaches pulls her from fortune's sight
Back to the huddled bed, Fay, Jamal clutch
      Warming on Mama leech-tight,
      And she cries at their touch.

But calm can't come from her tear,
      Flinches from Jamal they excite
      That elder burden, passed down fear:
Suffer suffering, it comes to her young
      Bent hard they'll disappear
      Under crosses that sour their tongue.

Mocked this moment, something she's known
      Comes like water on rain, severe,
      A hard inheritance—her folks, her own—
Comes by her three, their bit is placed
      Pulled fast; Mama sees, up alone,
      How much the summer storm debased.

She wants so bad to panic them away,
      Run, scramble out postpone
      Reckoning anything but stay
Here her children dripped with city spit, heave
      Over this place, at last betray
      Sheltering lies and leave.

But out by filth-dimmed walls
     Face it again, the way
     They'd whisper while she stalls;
Nothing, there it is, no in-case-
     Call, nothing but leering halls
     Christ, or this hollow place.

Mama knows there's nothing out but back,
     Down like deadweight falls
     Hands herself down to them slack,
Pockets the old pain;
     They help her rise when the patch fails
     Together raise cardboard against the rain.

For Tom Robbins

I

The heart's trouble.
It hardens, skips,
each spasm involuntary,
quite the independence-minded muscle
throbbing out of control;
and it stops, once
or twice in its great while.
But even then we miss the reverie
when its rhythm loses cue
and blood tides idle,
'cause the center that Jacob knew
checks out with our true mark of time
and, bowing, that fleshy metronome
lets us sputter solo.
Yet the heart gentle, leaves politely,
mute towards our forgetfulness
with no mock of how we missed the beat.

II

We are what we can't know.
Once God was that abyss, the not known,
but now we're that.
We can't explain the brain
so smugly snort, "That's us!"
But cry for the day that we tame the brain
and our nervousness tics within some formula—
unimpressed we'll fade
knowing too much to trouble with living.
Though then, the heart's revival
could be near for us the cerebrally bored,
but oh! could we rest simply
being the involuntary?

Sharon Clark-Burland

Framework

Something in my shoulders braces
in these walls,
strains to hear that pad of footsteps
down that hallway,
knows he is everywhere...everywhere...
Momma's stare cracks in panes,
jars free mortar of my brothers' flesh,
yet brick slams bone
against bone,
welds upright.
Someone still there
claws into my jaw,
grabs escaping breaths,
crouches beneath rage thickened bone,
hurt calcified to bone,
leaks a cold panic into muscles,
bursts screeching from my pores,
as my father's house collapses
onto its foundation,
by an ocean
that never knew
he'd built there.

Postpartum

What was it I feared
tip-toeing into the nursery
to slip finger beneath slight breaths,
huddled from the man rising
to watch from doorway,
waiting to claim this thickened body
snatched from flow of flesh,
widened from ever hardening back into form
among cold, dank sheets;
Sacred,
squat and crouched
far from rising in mountain streams
with gowns of water,
to dance now
only in moonlight
shining through parted drapes?

Why couldn't he do battle,
this father I shredded
for son,
forgotten in the long run
between work
and housework
and PTA,
letting me relegate him to walls
rising about us,
that sons could grow tall
alongside his length,
touching me as eldest child;
Sacred,
forever behind
closed nursery door,
flesh with
his flesh?

Gillian Conoley

Rush Hour

All day, the important things
leave. Behind the skyline,
the sun is a fast star.
Light seeps
into the city. The street lunges
on its silver belly, turns
back, gives up.
Up steel grids, the city's
last hot breath
pushes itself everywhere
like a stain. They start
to come out, the black suits, men
who can't wait
to loosen their ties. They brandish
briefcases like tense dreams that
just repeat and repeat. Women
exit buildings alone, their hands
shading their eyes, their hands cupped
like hats. Everyone is necessary.
At five o'clock, everyone
wants bourbon, or sleep. Sales
girls lilt past
with a smell of old gardenias, stiletto
heels clicking their song
like castanets. Nylon against flesh,
the swish of skirts. On streetcorners,
newspapers hide faces. Headlines
turn the world
into one small idea. The old drunk
propped on the corner
is asleep with a smile
on his face that could save
this city. Workers pass
him, think "misplaced brick."

The Cousin at the Funeral

Three in the afternoon,
                          my skirt
held up in one fist,
our grandmother not even cold, we waded
far down the river,
                    not stopping
until the tree moss
                      hung in sweeps
and there was shade. Even then
I thought of how
you would tell it:

                        years later, after making love
in a city,
          its noise clanging
below you, your lover
watching as you stare away from her
to speak. She strains

to see you then, the way
you must have looked,
                        tall in your suit,
and me, like you,
                    tanned and gangly
but a girl.

             You tell her
slowly, your voice carrying
                            until she begins to nod,
knowing the amber light,
the smell of the rotting trunks,
                            the glimpse of me, you,
lying there on the shore.

The Sound I Make Leaving

Always I am just returning in a blue dress,
tight and daring. You've come to see me
that way, tall and bringing
no objects. Through the anemic

twilight we drag
the weekend, wondering
if this town will stop or pull
its trigger. It's difficult:

42

looking for the linear
way to talk. I want to
stir the light of this room
from its slow fade, make our couch

a peninsula we could cling to,
let the window call
what won't come out of our mouths
until the neighbors
fall forward
from their porches
and the whole day is a question
we can't hear.

Woman Speaking Inside Film Noir

What I want happens
not when the man leaning on a lamppost
stares up to my room and I meet his gaze
through the blinds, but in the moment after,
in the neon's pulse, when his cigarette
glows in the rain like a siren
and he looks away.

I go back to bed and imagine
the sound of his shoes
on the wooden stairs, flight
after flight, my pincurls loosening,
falling across the pillow
gentle as dropped bolts of bargain silk.

When the door flies open there's nothing
but the luminous band of the radio,
still he steps toward me
in a pyramid of light.
Our shadows yearn across the dresser,
my perfume bottles glisten
like shots of scotch. The mirror
is one more stilled moon
that wants the wish of him,
his face upturned,
astonished, cloudy as opal.

Gary Cooper

Come With Me

Come with me now
  all you who want rain
    to where Parsifal, the single-minded
      the pure-hearted seer of God
    under a dry sky and no thunder
      fishes in a pool gone gray.
And watch with me
  as the rod bends sharp
  like a snake striking
and the fish rolls white and desperate
  the rod biting back
    once, twice, three times
      and again
until fish or angel
  fin or wing
   lies white and content
    in the sand at our feet
   breathing neither air nor water.
But still we wait the rain.
  So I take the rod
  and cast far out and deep
    into the dark water.

Crossing the Sound

I leave her and cross the sound from Seattle to Bremerton.
West in slanting light the water is gray slate.
Straight down beside the ferry it is black and deep.
I prefer the gray and reach out to the fisherman
so out of place riding the great swells
while salmon fill the black water
    rising and falling under us.

Then I am aware only of her,
far lovelier at forty than seventeen
like a salmon turning silver in the sea
near the river's mouth and the long run upstream.
And I'm afraid of her whose beauty touches me
too closely, who is at home in the sea,
afraid my fear will leave me, small man like all men,
    alone and night near.

In His Summer

In his summer, he waited
for steps too small to keep his stride
on trails climbing to lake mornings
and trout rising to spoons—rainbow splashings
under hills hallowed by the elk's bugle
and his great joy in them.
At night in a bag they made warm
the boy slept in his father's back
dreaming a winter river
and his father at the blue ice-edge
where the whitefish gathered to him
blessing and blessed.
Now, long awake to his own summer
alone on streams,
the boy still lifts the fish
green and silver-quick to the sun
to the bend upstream
where his father waits out of sight
drifting salmon eggs through pools so blue, so deep
they are forever.

I-90, Still Heading West

Those rivers in Montana
        they have enough of their own
                and never notice us.
And the fish that flash from their bottoms
        so open to the rain
                to leaves falling
        so patient with the ice
                and spring's sudden life—
        they don't need us.
But we can hardly care anymore
        who own neither fin nor claw.

So the March moon
        cold and careful in her ministry
                rides unattended
                        except for the geese,
        a morning pair, who after fitful circle
                heed her, correct their heading
                        and on glad wings turn north.

Tom Davis

A Great Day by God

These colors are healing: ash greens,
golds, desert plants in June.
My dripping nose knows
lubrication handkerchiefs
are wet for, but I snuff
it up and spit it vehemently
at the sand a couple feet
from where I strangle within
the sound of Hangman Creek.

Each plant stinks: yarrow,
a glib reminder, asthma,
mugwort pollen dust. Oh,
nature's on top in this.
These colors heal. These smells
decongest. This reminder:
if it's world: mosquito, gnat,
no see um, deerfly, ant breathing
easy, at least. Horsefly haloing
me chokes out the sound of
Hangman Creek.

Being Dangerous Alaska Style
For a Spokane Native

Port means drunk in Alaska
that deep red drink
guzzles up drizzle,
speaks angel in Tlingkit,
or spells disaster
at hands thirty foot waves
tinker with. Going north
for crab or fish, boats (the crews)
season at bars
where justice resides

in the face of raw egg
and "whoever's kid that is
sure looks like Didrickson; where
is Didrickson, now, anyway?"
Time resides in the jade face
of a wave the sun
irradiates 5000 miles
south. Natives are drunk
on something. They never
show it.

The Columnar Basalt
of Moses Coulee

The rocks grew slender: thin shafts—
lumped needles hurtling down debris, scree—
extruded as purged crystalline drabness
except for masses of yellow and red and turquoise
mosses like some oriental matting or medieval maps
of just dreamed peninsulas or isthmuses
bridging ocher continents lapped by seas
silkier than ice. Cut loose we drifted.

Madeline DeFrees

Driving Home

The wheels keep pulling
towards that sunny sideroad.
I pull them back, headed for Blue Creek.
Grasses getting thin, the rushes lean. Nothing here
the wind can use against me.

In the long stretch
after Cataldo takes the hill, I think about
Clarence Worth Love's annulment
till a nerve gives way.
The gradual curve unwinds
the river again. Now it is green in the placid
crook of my arm
as the paired hands of those days
I wanted to die.

By the Superior exit
the highway crew leaves markers
I do not trust. The diamond
watch for crossing game, for ice and rocks,
hangs a legend on my lights.
I do the same. One star is out to get me.

A level sound. Pastures graze the trees
around the shoulder.
On a high beam, the mare swings
her dark side to the moon.
Something turns over in the trunk.
I think
one more time
of your black luggage
on the bed. I know
it may not carry me much longer.

Extended Outlook

November days, and the vague shape of a wing,
of a claw at the sill, at the drawn
shade of the bedroom,
signals the oncoming freeze. Setting
the scent-baited trap for the shadow mouse
back of the dark pine cabinet,
the tenant hears the cat downstairs
whining to be let in.

               The tree is a violin bow
scraping the sound box of the house
all day. Close to the ribbed
breath, the scrolled end of wind under the eaves
turns back on the fine-tuned neck,
answers the shrill
jay in the caterwaul of blue
and falling light.

               Trying to score this weather
for strings, no hurricane, but a planned
diminuendo, I pretend that the house is my own;
the cat, my pet. That Canada
wishes me well. That the blue shriek and the wail
are a cradlesong and the gulf
repeating this gale in my ear, is an old friend
or no friend of mine.

Keeping Up with the Signs

Meadowlarks nesting March to August yield
to summer traffic in the dovetailed grass.
Three clear notes. Do Not Walk in Open Field.

I run the way my feet suggest. Upheld
by ringing turf and larkspur flash, I chase
meadowlarks nesting. March to August yield

sways heavy on the cornstalked land I flailed
to find the spot where larks come less and less.
Three clear notes do not walk. In open field,

runways the wind lays flat, fill up. Revealed
in the natural clutch called happiness:
meadowlarks' nesting March to August yield

in the tilt of wind, rainswell and the cold
mating ground, to bed with the dangerous
three. Clear notes do not walk in open field.

I leave five clues for the field guide whose wild
speculation turns the head. Shells express
meadowlarks' nesting March to August yield.
Three clear notes do not. Walk in open field.

Nights of Flint and Snow

fill with your long absence, the wind
not bitter,
ice, an age to come. When sky lets go
it is warm work digging you out,
headlight còld in the socket,
one branch of the cedar
down.

　　　The compost path
steepens on both sides of the summer-
house. I think of old mines
reopened: veins of chard,
sad pods in coal-dark seams, the golden load
unfolding in the buried ear. I ride the waves,
green, to the sea
warm rain.

　　　　Weathered beets. The seal-faced kelp
torn from its rank salt bed
and the puckered kiss
of anemone.

　　　　Water turns us back,
road and river curving under ice
to the deepening source. Home. Inside
your place is warm
plum and apple slowly turning wine.

Pendant Watch

In Missoula, Montana, where the townsfolk water
the sidewalks, and the Clark Fork River barely interrupts
the usual flow of traffic on Higgins Avenue, I pass,
outside a furniture store, the world's largest
captain's chair. In it sits the world's largest captain,
native to Montana, foursquare and friendly,
with a timeless eye trained on the University
while the mountain flashes holding heaven
in a mist the rest of us steer clear of.

Still agile at forty-odd, I could shinny up
that walnut leg to lie in the lap of the god,
call him husband or lover, warm as any woman in a clockwork
swoon. Except that some more concentrated fire balanced
the cogs, married gut to metal. Today's AP wire
ticks off: Nun Burns Self to Death, and in eight-point type
from Saigon, a Buddhist virgin goes out in sheer fire
while I splutter cold a spark at a time.

Time hangs golden at my breast, a decoration in disrepair
that may not run much longer. Still, I am there beside
that well-regulated throne or bed, not altogether dead.
And the captain knows. And I know. We have it timed to the second.

The Register

All night I hear the one-way door sigh outward
into billboard glare. The ninth-floor
cul-de-sac left by the wrecker's ball, my new
apartment.

           Inside the known hotel, decor of watered
silk and fleur-de-lis, the French Provincial
red-and-white, mine for the night, no more. A weak
bulb wears a halo through the dark.

                          The street
divides below the skid of rubber burning. One branch
leads to a hill's last word, one into morning.
Flying in place, hung from its thirst, hummingbird
in the honey throat of a flower.

                              Bless me,
Father, I have sins to spare and love
these relics of the hybrid years I spent afraid
to move. Chant of common life, field lilies, all
that labor, too cautious then to spin.
Not even Solomon would know these regal lily flowers,
translated fleur-de-lis my wall
provides, the glory flowers-*de-luce*, of light breaking
clean on the iris. I open
my eyes to the light.

                         Bless me, Father,
under heavy sun and hoping
still to make your life my own. I cannot nullify
the work this body's done
nor call each act religion. Wherever one road
joins another, blind, I think of you
and conjure up the loss. When two roads, gaining
speed, speed up to intersect, I cross
myself and lay the body down, arms open for what comes
to pass. Father, I am signing in.

Tumbleweed

Detachable. The mobile American par excellence:
rootlessness its survival, and the way
to permanence, an airborne transience
over dusty miles.
Gregarious in its origin,
perpetual distance wears it thin:
all sinew and fiber in a pulp-and-blossom world;
drier than sage
and less inclined to cling;
hollow as cactus but robbed of its reserves.
Not so dramatic, either, with shadow, spike and flower
crowning a hundred years with impossible bloom.

Tumbleweed lives by the day or less:
its route is rotary, its music, motion and it calls
from every river margin and wayside gulch
crying the wind *Take me. Of all this matted company*
most volatile and free!

Freer than feathery dandelion adrift on hum of bees,
heels over head in bed of violable clay,
weightless and waiting
it courts the fickle air.
Patient among reeds, its seeds accept the sand,
abide in evanescence,
calculate on chance.
Its vagrancy vaguely sanctioned by radical elements
and good for something surely:
synthetic cereal—
better than seaweed! An active vegetable.

Tumbleweed, restless and windblown,
rises on breezy rhetoric to unspectacular flight
out of the billboard jungle,
out of the closed, airtight
cells of civilization
into the open plain: useless and fruitless,
homeless, helpless, lost
to dignify Becoming sprung from dust.

Anita Endrezze

One Thing, Too Much

We all love one thing too much,
Chocolate. Coffee. Liquor.

We all love one man too much.
He is too close.
Or too far away.
Or we haven't been introduced yet.

We all fear one thing too much.
Being alone. Dying.
The stranger at the door.

We all lose one thing too much.
Our hopes, the long needles
of desire, the resilient cheek.
We all think we know too much:
our neighbor's business,
our children's secrets,
how a rose unfolds from memory.

But we don't know
what our own backs
look like
unless we're willing to see
from a different perspective.
We don't know that the stranger
is the lover we've always waited for.
We don't know that death
is the way
we shake hands
with life.

We don't know that too much
of one thing
is like a burning woman
calling for more wood.

The Language of Fossils
(Vantage, Wa.)

this desert is a plateau of light

small diggers live in the soft stone
tongues of ancient beasts

calcified waves *stillflow* under
the sulfur-bellied marmots
and badgers claw at the salty star-
fish that tremble into dust

these stone logs are only weathering
time, waiting
for the Cascades to become ash
and the ocean's green winds
to transform the sky
into acres of ferns

what will we become?
cool shadows in the red
mineral belly of the earth?

fossils speak the language of *Ginkgo*:
vowels like flat stones
with the carbonized wings
of leaf and beetle
and consonants like a bone
caught in the earth's throat

diceratherian:
rhino pillowed in lava
layers of basalt bone
calcite dolomite pyrite
strates of chalky diatoms
agate flint chert

what language is my passing
shadow? my name is lost
off the Columbia's cliffs:
immersed in silica and water
it will become an opal
with a woman's soul

The Medicine Woman's Daughter:
A Charm to Keep You Part of the Whole

May the white bark be nine times your mother
May my burnished cheeks be twice sun-daughters
May the apple that divides seeds into simple stars
        be the multiple of your life
May my breasts be the marigolds in your night garden
May the dark broom that is your shadow be a memorial to your father
May you live between my thighs and in my heart
May lapwings rise at your feet from every cross road
May I be between your two hands the way sky is the center
        of beech dreams
May our love be the mystery of wind and the soul's duration
May your life be as charmed, as strong, as the single white
        rose blooming in snowy circles

Ways to See

1

a waterfall is one way river sheds its skin
a boiling pot is the steam's cradle song
the black night is what's left of weather-eaten stars
the flowers are the way the dead see

2

I hardly know myself anymore
my hands are two place mats at an empty table

I follow strangers, looking for your face
I wander, untouchable desire,
a ghost with passionate skin
a beautiful lost body

3

here's the pity: the self
which sees only loss

4

and yet with my desolate lips, I drink
from the dry pot that scorches the minerals
I know the skin that receives nothing but the dusty caresses
of stars
I see the night dispersing into the dark branches of water

5

in my hair, a dried flower that seeks my moist oils
in my mirror, the face of a woman
    who sits down to drink from an empty bottle
    to stare at the river's dry shadow
    to see the minerals in her eyes give depth to her grave face
    to find the night entering darkly through the mouth
and to know, Oh, the sad ways the heart boils dry

Tina Foriyes

Idaho Vaudeville

In July on an afternoon ride
it is memory that maps the slow drive.

    You see as through old glass,
how buildings hunker to the land, and
log slouches back on weathered log;
while across the graveled road, vertical boards
spider a new and rising shape
into the wide Idaho sky.

    Here what is remembered is lived.
How father taught daughter to mushroom
the stand of timber his father named
and, by evening, at the same farmhouse,
surrounded by porches and four-wheel rigs,
tubs of cold water swim with morel.

On every sill, old bottles,
glass perennials unearthed during repairs,
grow green cuttings, filaments to light
the winter eye;

               and the large black fly
that buzzed in the bathroom, now angles
a path in the pane above the kitchen sink,
where the dishwasher swathes plate
after unmatched plate, and watches
the white mare and the appaloosa
spot the flank
of a cloud-mottled
hill.

In the front yard
a dog rises
and recognizes friends.

Their hands
vase
wildflowers:

lupine,
ladyslipper,
fireweed.

With the ease of air
they cross the open doorway,

the wood floor under their boot
undulates
like the Palouse.

Conversation wears a vaudeville face
humor with the lag of the land,
you hear how

in the hot climb of a hill
the combine freed itself of the tractor
and rolled toward the edge of the ridge:

      "Over the cliff?"
      "No-o," speaker replies.
      "Oh, good. What stopped it?"

      A clearing of throat becomes a caliper of meaning.

      "The grain truck."
            Burlesque laughter and beer,
      someone musing, "How?
      In all that field space!"
      receives the remark,
         "Idaho comic relief."
         And one by one,
the sky,
framed above the sink,
calls each
by their own color
to the west porch
where the woman-shaped hills

repeat

      "Wheat
      is but a grain
      in the harvest of this place."

Run-Off

As the lake fell into place
each February behind the house
when the rain ran the creek to overwash its banks
and the melting snow rushed down from the rounds of hills,
an inevitability settled on her,

and a moon settled in the backyard.

A scent of sea things shifted in the air,
as she watched from the sun-deck turned widow's walk
and listened to the river that runneled the eaves;

the house turned ship,
ship unmoored.

Sadie's Elegy

In the darkest corner of the yard,
up close to the drive where I park the jeep,
she'd pressed a hollow in the grass through the years,
blending her black to the shadows of night and house,
only her age-white muzzle
eventually gave her away,
                        and only to my knowing eye.

The grass has stopped growing.
November is snowless, but colder this year;
and here, a month after she staggered breathless at dawn
to that corner to die,
                    the grass is flat to my eye,
                    and leaves have begun to gather in that hollow.

When in Drought

That summer she could not guess at goodness
and be surprised. Driving out of it,
she would always remain unsure
of the year, of the day of week,
of the specific unhappiness.

Her reality was emotion; her calendar,
the seasons. Abstinence and lack of rain
had centered her in thirst.

Hoping that motion and change would be solution,
she drove south to Grangeville,
consciousness closing on the heat gauge
and the plowed-under fields
where, right and left, smoke rose from the dirt
as though from secret fire.

Sun simmered from the open metal of the jeep,
cupped from the sky,
and she did not need a mirror
to see that she was burning.

It was after 3—in a landscape with no more shade
than the penciled shadow of a fence post—
that she came upon the farmer's homescrawled billboard,
"Praise the Lord, anyway"
and she parked in the comfort of its words.

Joan Fox

Fugitive

First it was the citizens
who came to me,
a widow of revolution
burning for it alone in her bed,
I used to get big men, police
back from a manhunt, heavy
and quick on me, these men

slept easy and late
in the mornings they questioned me
as I pressed
my hands in the linoleum
waiting for the toast to brown
they wanted a scapegoat
and I was easy
they thought I shared their motives and plans,
But lies are their own affair
when they leave and give me a pat on the ass

I forgot them then, still
mostly I was willing
until one night a new man
who didn't have heated breath or blood
under his fingernails, who smelled
like the ocean
I wished to live by
I could see he was alarmed by my past
he led me by the hand to my bedroom
tugging me through every hallway
he opened the window and pine needles blew
he rolled me over once on my bed and came
to see me standing in the wind
then he asked if,
with a sad laugh he pulled me down and
kept me there for days
our skin echoed out the doors
his voice groaned in my ear
finally he let me sleep

in the morning I wake
and can't find this man
or my house
but this new house has paint threads
peeling from its sides
glass pinches my skin
if I start to cry

now at the edge
where ocean strips sand dry
through the hours with gentle flutters
the tide pools empty and come swaying
into the kitchen hugging my shins
sucking corners so close
to the sea I roll out of bed into driftwood
I am in a new place with every breath
combing algae through my hair
when my house is as much sand as wood
the strangest men start to visit me,
with shuttered eyes and tangy sweat,
I can't stand how their smells
tighten in my throat
—I make them bathe in the sea
after they come back sweet
with the rubber smell of salt,
they only ask for coffee
and they leave

while it's still dark, I ask them
if they know this man, the man who hides
from love, ask them if they know where
he hides,
and finally,
when I think my tongue aches
too much I ask again
one night I am answered
from a man wearing half a handcuff
sweating rust
and licking his prison tattoo
as if it were a wound he could
heal like a cat
he stares
at me and hands

me camouflage
I lift, place this skin
round, shadowing
my neck a sea snake,
writhing under the pulse
of half-formed whisperings
am I to suppose it is from my man?
Now I wonder if love makes a point
between being and hiding
I swim deep in the ocean.

Philip Garrison

Frames

Elbow grease put my grandfathers in gold
frames, on coffee tables in the suburbs.
While other families grease someone's palm,
we, elbows like pump handles, gush hard work.

Aunt Leora dug a well by hand.
Plain, sly, raining handshakes,
my father called on customers—
it was a living.

Me, I'm tickled there
is something left out
the window to describe, now
I'm middleaged.

The eaves drip. It is
all I have worked for.

*

O my clothes, hanging in the closet,
even, you look restless, anywhere
but on me.
Sleeves dark tunnels I reach down gingerly.
Pantlegs wrinkled from running after subways.

I think of you even when fixing lunch.
Slicing the huge pink tongue straight
to formica, click. And chewing
meditatively, and chewing

watching Eric Sevareid, the sound
off, Bach on FM.
And Eric moving his jaw slowly, as if in pain
entering the living room of someone
in old, deep-fitting clothes

I leave you twisted on the floor
the night I come home drunk. And leave you
washed and ironed hanging in the closet
the next night. Though I lie hungover,
limp, unable to move, o my clothes

you have outrun the poverty color
fast in you, and wait for me
with holes in your pockets.

*

Hermes, I never could bluff
past you. In the Metropolitan Museum,
around the corner
from the Roman bodybuilders

you watched everyone stay the same
for wear. But it was one hard winter.
But I drank it under control, thanks
to Ernest and Julio Gallo and
approximately 800
B.C., some stonecutter getting lonesome.

Every day there you were,
a little stone kid
legless with anticipation.

*

Suddenly, it isn't too late. Suddenly
I can shuffle the shovel's width of dirt
I stare at, in or out, blinking

each ant and crack downhill,
to, there, isn't that, better?
She rolls over. She wanted a cigarette

a moment ago. Now she has one
of the world's great smiles on,
and polka dot panties. And wonders

do I think of her when I come.
Now daylight, slowly, releases
foothills a day's walk away.

from the Fantods

2. Adelita, from Spokane

Out on one edge of the continent,
where a stagecoach paused
90 years ago, and stores sprang up,

among fields twitching like horse skin
tonight, I glance over both shoulders.
They feel like hogs, on a Mexican curb, singing

from knife and bloody quarter nelson,—
the men I clasp between shaved legs.
They call different names at the wallpaper.

My least pause thrills
from the hairy ribs one
note, exact, and untranslatable.

Once, I couldn't remember
was it *que horas son?*
or *corazon.* We married,

and made that damn mobile
home quiver with each other,
till one morning I came in with diesel fuel on my nylons.

Wallpaper went transparent
with our flashy final present
tense of each other,

and leaves showed through granite.
My bus shuddered at a highway.
Mere bits of gravel tarred to granite

broke earth's surface tension,
fender slipping by cutbank,
by hay stacked on cactus...

O my gradual departure,
doorways cast down light for you.
Even windowpanes.

4. Copenhagen Tins

He flat wouldn't leave,
one eighty year old man,
before Mt. St. Helens blew.

So can you figure how, that
dumb, he got that old?
By being just as tough as you

are, my metal blossoms, my arroyo
flash flood of cans.
You bloomed in hip pockets.

You fell fragrant from the truck
windows of lonely men
who'll not be coming back

ever. Now you snuggle
doorknob fashion into the palm
of a woman

bending by the road:
she wears a flowered housecoat.
She drags a gunnysack.

And all those old bastards feel
like they're hidden in her, eyeing her
and spitting and winking.

Lynne Haley Slaughter

Conconully

There in the dryland snake country one burned hill
like any other might slope down to find Lake Conconully
cricket seeded, making its broad water sound the valley
hoards like news of breath or fortune

At the cabin Aunt Agnes turned from glass
her pincurled hair identified her
like an oak's whorled grain: every ring
a spurt of life, each knot a missing branch
Aunt Agnes thin and rippled, whittled down

Uncle Kurt knew secret roads and pounded us
through ruts toward fishing holes, roads which climb
high above the lake, block its view with scrub brush
Okanogan cliffs you can't get close to

But behind the cabin steer bones marked
the certain hill too steep for cattle, worth
scratched hands to climb late evening when sun
cools, where the summit shows grey water curving
to the farther hill, new dermis gleam, one rowboat
fast within its center, one fisherman in bloom

Geothermal

> "It is not the sun of the outer world that we see here. It
> is another sun—an entirely different sun—that casts its
> eternal noonday effulgence upon the face of the inner
> world."
>
> —Edgar Rice Burroughs
> *At the Earth's Core*

Somewhere in those hills the light makes wildflowers
come, dull roots feed on that desert's center
as on nitrogen, a pinpoint where the whole earth
steadies and draws in, where my heart is drawn

Bare soil conceals what summer months might tell
if you knew the signs; beyond one barrier
elk feed, beneath scrub blossoms life begins
and has no breadth and does not weaken

There, earth's hollow center fills and centuries
cannot be reckoned, there is nothing you might hold
within your hand; an intelligence unfound beams
its language to our hopeless cells

And in the sky the desert menaces, its dust
stopped atoms, keeps apart; it is too small
A speck of color on one hill distracts the eye

The hours make us beg each second breath and touch
our pulse; we keep apart, our earth-bond only seconds
when feet press, makes us bleed mid-stride
It is too small, this hour, this breath

Nespelem, Colville Reservation

There is a canyon at the river's bend
where sun stops in its circle of the world
where air has no oxygen, lungs no expansion
where the water runs vermillion

Barren soil sustains, blighted fields
conceal visions: Bitterroot, camas, lomatium
I would gather in the early hours
move my hands as light moves
glean what only comes to women

Spirit of the dream, my times
are close and hollow; strung beads
have no middle, united I am unfulfilled
Show me the circle of the world

Sing me the small names of those earthchips
unwind the words which spoken mean life
uncoil what will not come,
unearth soil sealed by death, secrets
rolled about the grave as if across the tongue

Mark Halperin

Early October with Cows

Across the field, stacks of hay-bales bulge
   from the rectangle of my neighbor's
   propped with a jiggery of poles.
Cows that appeared by the fence one day
last Spring, skittish, fly-ridden,
   lower their eyes and go on
eating. Leaves rattle; long grasses rub

like insects' legs that hummed summer along.
   More cows are coming, black
   and white with thickening hides
and fat slobbering tongues, the afternoon's
few drowzy bees. The sun rakes leaves,
   its low slant across the field,
red on the stacks of tottering hay. Soon

it's too cold to sit outside, too loud
   once the crows begin to mob.
   An owl repeats the wind, a gate
the loose click and grate of the earth
turning. The cows drift toward winter,
   small, heavily laden ships
rolling slightly in the chop and swell.

A Song of the Autumn

The clear wings of the mayflies
turn to slate. You hear the cricket
counting more slowly and a stillness
amplify the sound. As you sit

a mushroom lifts its head. A pearl
from a dim world clambers
into this one. A dead stump
sprouts with strangely soft flowers.

Deepening, the Autumn is its haze.
The stray men you chance on
as you travel the backroads, linger,
talking with you through the afternoon.

Now if the frost destroys your garden
and an innocent sadness should weigh
on you like their forgotten names,
you can accept it. You will say:

the world is not a human place
though we live here. Now the shedding of the tree.
Now the woodchuck crawling underground.
You will not look for special mercy.

Logger on the Upper Klickitat

He's pissing in the V formed by the door
of his open cab, a stack of logs chained
in the forks. His gaze is distant, as though he saw
on the horizon, maybe a hint of rain,

a wisp of smoke. As he zippers up, I say:
"I heard in Klickitat there was a road
by the river, near the St. Regis Paper Company
stacking yard—you wouldn't happen to know it?"

Flies buzz in the dust. His scan is down
on my waders, below the bright steelhead flies,
below the dangling net. I catch him frown
as he climbs into the truck. I feel his eyes

crossing toward me. "It's the left fork, that way.
It goes through Yakima land. The reservation
starts a mile on." "They wouldn't mind, would they?"
"Sometimes they'll chase you if you're there alone,"

he says, watching my friend; and deep colors
fan his cheek. "I never heard a two white men
having trouble," and faster, "whipped them cocksuckers
once, guess we'll have to teach 'em again."

The Deaths on Hayward Hill

My neighbor breathes in deeply, and I suppose
it is the dead dog, the dead and injured sheep
he thinks of, and the herder to be paid.
At the top of Hayward Hill we stand
outside a makeshift pen. Two dozen ewes
huddle, rocking drowsily like boats.
Clear fluids gather at their bloody necks
and drip. Across the road the rams watch,
amble toward the fence to lie down,
round side by round side, a frieze
in the halls of the final courts of judgment.

All day I have struggled against sleep;
now I give in easily. I imagine
the dead dog as he sails forward in a pure
brutality of play whose outcome will be
the death of sheep, but free of the mildest rancor.
Again he rises higher in the arc.
This time he turns, as though called, and the lead
burns through his side.
The maimed sheep hang their heads, the purple
of their raw flesh, robes in the kingdoms of pain.
I need to believe joy also has its power.

Travels

Some calm, frosty morning like today's,
when I am tempted to ask where I have been,
in or away from myself, with a hint at
my sense of hovering, let me recall
the colorful cities, exotic as the reds
on the ground and bone white grasses:

the blues Migal, San Blas, Petrovoretz.
the many grays of boulevards in Barcelona,
gold lions on a bridge in Leningrad
and the pinks that dotted Jalapa's rainy terraces.
I have been further than I dared hope—
to Kiev and Marseille and Jerusalem, cities

like tattered robes in which the world
has swirled its history. That morning—
should the year drag toward an end as I divide
what I thought I chose from what I know
was imposed, luck against skill, work versus
accident—let me remember Oaxaca's market stalls

packed beside each other, red and black squares,
crammed with spices, and the tilting scales.
Or Yalta, the Black Sea's glistening, impossible
backdrop for hand-piled potatoes and stunted beets,
rows of pasty women in babushkas, expressionless
until their small scales begin to sway, until

fresh puff-bread and the smells of the bakers
wreathe all they wrap and sell. Remind me of
my wife calling, at the far end of the field
an eagle perched in the top of a wintery tree
where, white head and white tail, it may be all
that has been or ever will be stolen from eternity.

Wes Hanson

Judgment

Jim Sorenson rolled his shirt cuffs
    up his thick arms
    and grabbed the hardball
    before we roared out like Marines
    going to recess,

    where we chose sides,
    standing like chickens
    checking our toes,
    as Jim and Dale Stern
    picked friends
    destined for the Hall of Fame.

I watched some wandering ants
    walk the trench
    Tim Bird toed for home plate.

At last, Jim picked nearsighted Willy Mills,
    and I was left
    for Dale,
    who pointed at me

    while Jim stamped his hard ash bat
    on to a single ant.

Then their white knuckles
    climbed the bat.

Dale boomed out, "Eagle claws!"

Listening

My phone-wife oscillates around the receiver,
    talks   listens   adjusts her tone.

Over here I sit with earplugs in, reading,
    indoors   calm   indoors.

I read, "But the ears of the Beaver within were distracted
    by tappings upon his wall. . . ."

And my thinking films me squatting
    beside a rippling pond
    watching the beaver's paddling tail
    as he floats slender trees.

I snap a twig.

Down he slides
Then up inside
    indoors   safe   indoors.

Last winter, when things slowed,
    the beaver thought of toppling poplars.
Woven in his dome of twigs,
    he curled like a child under a pillow, hidden,
    indoors   still   indoors.

My oscillating phone-wife
    talks   listens   says goodbye.

Here I sit
    with my ears plugged, reading,
    "The Beaver knew. . . his heartbeat. . . . The sound was just
    as it should be."

The receiver clicks.

My phone-wife murmurs,
    Do you still have those earplugs in?

Indoors   here   indoors,
    I gnaw one earplug out.

James R. Hepworth

A Short History of Idaho

Begin with a few trappers lost in fur.
Name a lake *Henry,* a town *Fremont,*
another town *the woods.*

Now, very quietly, very, very quietly,
someone whisper

gold

Autumn in Inchelium

Autumn is cold in Inchelium.
Dark comes early, and although
I do not know the name for the season
in Salish, still, it is pleasant
to walk by the Trading Post
just as the electric lights come on
and to stare inside the huge windows.

Elsewhere, carcasses hang from porches—
snow powdered thick in the fur
of the mule deer. Somewhere far away,
a phonograph plays a love song.

Each night the moon and I hunt this field
and fall in love with the earth.
Nobody enjoys the assassination
more than the hired killer. If you
should find me bent over books
inside my window, do not be mistaken:
I'm not always looking for ways
to impart the works of men. Most often
I search for a means to destroy them.

Sketches: Colville Indian Reservation, 1975

1.

sings! Crying James who among other things
smells
like so many people who do not bathe
often
his nose misshaped the bridge
squashed flat into the broad skull
flat!
for a quarter the dumb beast
will cry for you—less if you are
white
such a man has a purpose

2.

rooted in the locale at forty
Crazy Quill wrinkles his nose
into an intricately stitched brown pillow
tightly the skin clings to his jowls
his iron-grey head hurries past
a lady in mink
dodging the clerk and disgruntled manager
Quill dives into his baggy pants
and gleams, "Teacher! Teacher!
Here is the five I borrowed for wine
last fall"—this in the spring
at J.C. Penney's

3.

galip-galump go the days
while stoic Modesta waddles
her Aunt Jemima build about
the shabby house grumpy
among the sparse furniture
in & out in & out
the screen door slaps
she is gone from the kitchen
drying bear meat on the rack
when I pull up the drive
a pack of nine full-grown dogs
come to greet me
meek I am afraid to get out
paw-prints all over the windows
Modesta glares and goes inside
the choppy barks are deafening

"What do you want?"
"I'm from the school. I..."
"What's wrong?"
"Nothing, I..."
"I send my girl to school
because it is the law.
I obey the law!"
Slams the screen door to my face

4.

absurd the pines the spruces the hemlocks
the moral in the wind dies there
and the clap takes a fifteen-year-old boy
to death the little Ignoble savage
yet there is a quiet beauty in the landscape
that profits the soul
or in the mind of aging Madalin
who married a French half a century ago
ninety years stoops she—
mouth permanently set—
corrects the linguist from Montana:
"In Salish the word you sayed
means 'bo-shit' but thass alright"
she giggles, "you are learning good.
I'm tired now. I think I'll go to bed.
Goooooooooooooood night. Gooooooooooood night."

5.

Rousseau! you slobbering imbecile
the people marry poor
die poor   bitterness

to beat hell out of the day
lovers spawn in the shadows
by the lake race their flashy cars
up and down the highway
until the blur of dawn

Christopher Howell

Exclusivity

Orchestral September. The prime
insect quadrillion finish one movement
and crash into the next, mad
with the sexual sweetness of what they are saying.
High in darkened oaks
or along the dipping stems of shrubberies
they pipe an ecstasy even the moon could hear
if moon would listen once; if once
she weren't so much the queen
of purest darkness out beyond where sound can go.
So what; the moon has no crickets,
no katydids. So
the moon just watches ripples
of music rising off the lips of the atmosphere,
vaguely stroking her
gravitational tether until, saddened, she seems to burn
a little brighter. Which is what September means
to the insects. I remember
touching you, rubbing
you slowly with this brightness,
the brightness of time. You sang,
I remember, just as the night, because it is the moon's friend,
wished you to, just as the moon does
sing; though we can't hear her.
We can only feel.

Like Feelings

Moonlight is all over the sycamores
and down the street singing
like a drunk.
It's all over my dog and me, too,
stepping out our evening's amble
among the crickets and parked cars,
couples murmuring on porch swings.
It is fifteen years
we've been doing this
walking the night streets
pleasantly fried by dreams lifting
everywhere along the elm boughs
and it is inside us now
like feelings
that bloom open as we move
so that finally we are out of reckoning
smoothly
richly filled, like jars, with all our nights
and walks together
and nothing spills or shatters this.
An angry shadow from an alley leaps
and shoots us
and we just step out of our bodies
and go on.

"That's life,
thank God" (mine and the god of dogs) I don't
tell him, or you, or anyone.
And I don't say I've got the pain of it
shut off or that I've buried my last
deceit. After all, it's just the dog
listening
as things gleam and lumber in the rows
of darknesses
and what *is* there to day
to him?
I could unhinge the old
existentialist saw
about the sanctity of moments.
I could promise him a bone when we get back
then break my promise just to show
the waywardness of speech and truth.

Or I could tell him love is like the air
sometimes
and vice versa; which is to say, all there is
to live on.
But he knows that.

Poem Based on a Chinese Character Meaning, "A Fire to Notify Heaven"

Don't let it go out. Who knows
what godly face will find us
if you can just keep shining in the stacked
and roaring angles near the edge
of some bluff above the sea
or on an isle in a pit of the sea itself.
Don't let it go out. Prometheus
worked so hard for it and Epimetheus
suffered the horrors of Pandora, becoming
a kind of Los Angeles, for that exquisite theft
of the Sun's stepchild. And both of them
are with us, chained
in us, still
perfect likenesses of our daring to love light
and the gift and take of flames dancing
while they eat. Anyway, don't let it go
the way you feel yourself beginning to
flicker and starve
for perfection, which is God's alone
and is the only fuel that will hold the fire
or your form in it
safe while a vast attention rummages the planets
for that single beacon kept and keeping
faith.

The Toad Prince

Stolen things; the mosslight
lovely in a certain swail of dry birch leaves,
glittering and touched densities
touching back; her thicket
where the legs departed each
from each for starless depths of pleasure.
He would get them

into a jewelry box or a palm
of pocket and he would say, "This
is all you are, now,
I'm sorry. I needed the space," knowing
they knew the good lie finally out
with others, walking and dying
of the prisoner's garage sale optimism.

They would kill him, in the end,
of course, and lift, ethereally
through his vacant shape reclining on a lily.
Did he mourn that shape's prissy lack of lust?
No no no. He saw the beautiful prince
would hoard all transformation (simply
refuse to) but would take the kisses anyway
and keep on taking.

The Physics of Oh

My friend the hostage
of zero, dying of moon and red smoke
in her wrists, pumps and primes the ore of deviance
and it glitters its nests, nakedly awake
miniatures
hoping for hope. I shake, saying this, thinking
of her descent
back through the diamond gloves my hands make
wearing her breasts.

Ne peux-tu prendre les etoiles?
I arch and dive into the liquid hole
of this question, though I speak less French
than it does. How many zeros like this
can you count, holding yourself up,
painted egg, checking the glow of afternoon
(has it survived gravitation and the sticky maps
of history). Can you think of my friend
inside your face
both whole and empty, trapped
in the hypothetically infinite limit of your mouth
forming "oh?"

Marc Hudson

Okanogan Sleep

for Jody Wyatt

At dusk, Horn Hill
turns ruddy as a torch,
nighthawks swing out over the San Poil
and, when they dive,
that bass thrumming note is like a door
opening in the wind.
I have heard it before, often.

Night, and the moon is spinning
from its substance
a thin cloud
like the mantle of an ammonite.
Blue-white Vega burns near the zenith;
that high ancient meadow
mirrors this one—
bugloss, mullein, the red-orange of Arcturus
like a berry of Viburnum.
In this sparse land
sky is the greatest plenitude.

In certain of my dreams
the animals remove their masks
and are human;
the yellow pine, the fir
show their rings,
even sky is simply a man
of great reserve.

So sleep is a kind of walking
that takes me far
into the tamarack of Dugout Mountain,
the cool, glacial stands there
flaring more brightly as winter comes on.

Summer, Aeneas Valley

It is hard to face these hills
and not feel the thirst of being
in a dry land. Crumbling rock
like loaves too long in the sun,
yarrow easily bundled into a rushlight,
and lichen—green-gold beards of it
minutely branching on the deadfall,
dark, forking Cladonia on the bald summits—
these petrify
like the husks old stars give off.

Life is water
and the San Poil now
is but three steps across;
three steps more of aspen and alder
you face these baked hills,
the thick-barked ponderosas,
sparse, white-yellow grass
that already seems half flame.
Here a tree, a barred owl,
or a man without water
in a few days belong to the same species
of dust, adobe, and straw.

Voices Overheard on a Night
of the Perseid Shower

Our being here was brief.
We too lay in the burnt grass
and counted those stars
like wind-borne thistle seed;

of a dusty afternoon,
gathered mussels from the San Poil—
where the aspen shadow was deepest
there we found them
like the beaks of nestlings;

and marveled at the caddis fly,
that strange donkey
hauling its cairn
under the stream.

Yarrow, pearly everlasting
become like straw this time of year,
and the mullein, with its torch bearing seed,
its great tongues of goat wool,
dies back to a whorl of earth.

Better than you we understood
hardness under the grasses,
the long, long aprons of talus.

Rock flakes because of iron,
like blood drying into crusts
resembling lichen—

those plants have no memory
and must loosen the memory
even from stones
where seed or blood has fallen.

Winter, Aeneas Valley

The five parapets of Horn Hill
are dusted with snow; by the river
yellow doors in full sunlight
break from their hinges, the eyelids
of the aspen struck clean off.
Maybe the ledges of schist,
maybe they with their bundles of lichen,
their silvery weeds like brittle stars,
are as disinterested as they seem,
but the valley is thinning out.
At night the goat path
swings up the tableland toward Capella.
A manlike figure
shades his eyes and then steps out
the way the moon does early on,
not sure yet of its footing.
Because of the legends of wheat,
bread for the asking in the winter sky,
life always wants this elsewhere
and breaks free when it can.
As for us who remain,
we can pick the black moss from the branches
for our cakes and, under the broken ridge,
admire the talus of the leaf-shaped stones—
no more and no less than the poverty
rightfully ours in the end.

Christiane Jacox Kyle

Oracle

I drive all night; on my right the Great Bear
wheels and winds backwards like a restless eye.
Already old, the moon slides down the sky,
a late aurora sheathes the northern air.

I think of blind seals plummeting to where
blind waters sweep the lashes from their eyes.
Measure that distance. What can sanctify
the will to wander the moon's dark side? I swear

once there were those who knew how to live
in this world, drawing great shapes on bearskin
or damp walls: huge birds with hooked wings, a deft spear
lodged in a rib, each an amulet to give
a shape to fear. I explore the sky. I begin
with the first letter. The word is fear.

Six Poetry Anthologies
in the High School Library

for Tucker

Look here: pencilled between the thin
blue lines, his name, already smeared,
cancels the clean, white space in the margin

for *homeroom, date due,* the last year
he came to school. He'd stare at the ceiling,
his black eyes billowing with fear,

his hand tilted across a page, a wing
dragged down a steep alley-way
where I couldn't follow, or bring

my words to tame his fear. So I turned away
from his bent gait, the steady stink of beer,
and left him at the blackboard each day

while the factory hummed in his ears.
Gears he could understand, but the click
of words kept slipping from the soft sphere

of his mouth, and all he'd do was lick
thin air, stare at me, and wheeze
like dying birds might do, caught in the flick

of wheels. But what was he doing with these
thick anthologies? What dark wings pitched
in a dark night, and with an eagle's ease

Moving in undulating arches, stitched
the widest sky? He's been dead two years;
they found him splayed in a roadside ditch—

Now the thin, white lines of gravestones disappear
in winter. I curse the son-of-a-bitch
who left him there. One by one, I burn each card, sear
his name, and keep the tongue of my secret fear.

Sunday Afternoon

Because I am neither wife
nor lover, I contain my hands,
let one cradle my forehead
as I would cradle yours;
the other drops to my knee,
kneading the round bone, stiff
from sitting at this odd angle.
You do not have to say
this talk makes you tired,
or that the woman you should love
and the woman you do,
are not the same. Yawning,
you blame a cold drizzle
in the middle of May. Outside
the window, forsythia bloom
like impetuous girls
and I contain my thoughts
as I would fold your thin arms
into mine. Because I am neither
brave nor foolish, I do not say
what I want. You are gruff
with your son, and the rain
is like a mute hand at the window.

The Second Language

I walk through the classroom blazing with light.
In those hills beyond our one window the sun
has burned off the last of the morning fog. Already
it is October: Arabic, Japanese, Mexican, Yapi,
the students' eyes are careful as they write.

"Tell me," one asks, "what is the word for the sound
of quiet the forest will make?"
        "Quiet," I say.
"But if the quiet is full of sound, birds, trees
in the wind, water falling?"
       He is describing a man
and a woman, how he imagines their life to be.

"We have no word for that silence," I answer,
and I think of the hundreds of words we have
no word for: *simpatico, agape, hesed, nada,*
and the hundreds of homes where a man or a woman
returns each day, tired of work, tired
of the world, and has no word to come to
that means the quiet the forest makes saying
I am alive.
     So the child in his far room cries,
the wind cries, the pots rattle in the kitchen,
the wind rattles the bedroom where the man
and the woman lie, locked in the anger of their lives.
And the silence between them is a thin scream
that splits open the terrible round silence
of the rising moon, and the light spills over the hills
where the fog lays down its head and sighs.

And the man thinks of the desolate grey walls
of his work, and the woman thinks of the grey faces
of her students who are American. What country
is this, the moon dragging the horizon, rumbling
its great and broken weight into the breast
of hills, hush of sky, hush of tender trees,
of stars brittle to the touch, the bears dancing
in the northern air. In a far room the child
cries and they go to him.
                                        There moonlight
blankets his body, his arm flung over his head
in sleep, the way a fisherman flings all
he is in a single cast into a pool where fish,
bright as sudden stars, lie dreaming
amid the rocks. The mother and father
will gather the child clothed in light:
the hush of wind, song, stars will take them,
and their eyes will remember, their ears will hear
the words of the forest breathing its dream:
it will be a language before the moon
tore itself from the earth, the confusion of vapors,
the redolent splendor of dust in the spheres.

What is the word. What is the word. Hush. Hush. Hush.
We are learning a language that has no words,
of leaves, of laughter among the leaves, an earth spinning
homeward through the broken heart of the spheres.

Eric Johnson

Games

The game within
          the game

i.e. as I faced
the firing squad
they asked if I
preferred a blindfold
or a cigarette
I asked if they would please
light me on fire
as I did not
smoke.
Local ordinances
prevented them
from burning.

Poem for a Friend

You understand this
is not a poem
but a frame
but no canvas
do I paint myself in
but corners to
coroners
do I go
all rotted with life
the good as well as bad
I haven't the ear
for poetry
you understand,
I go from one paralysis
to the next
not sending comfort
but finding it.

Someday

I will take you to the
                dark school

A darker school than
           you have ever learned

Though perhaps once upon a
time you tried to teach it

and many a teacher can
teach that which he had never
                learned to do or become

Someday to the dark school
we will go

and fall down the dark
corridors

and burn as our heart
stops and our lungs burst

and only a pinprickle bubble
in our brain lives

Someday I shall take you
to the dark school

That I alone have lived
to hear and breathe

and tell of

Thorns

While my
rose slept
I dreamt of
thorns
and slept with
one under
my skin
as the roselight
pulled me away
from my heart
and toward
the sky
above

93

William Johnson

Digging Spuds

We get up early
and walk out into the patch, husks
like a blownover orchard
blasted with frost.
I fork up the clumps
while my son peels the cake
from their leathery hides
and we toss them in heaps on the lawn.
They're dufflebags lost in the mud,
tired misshapen footballs
happy just to be alive.
We sack them in burlap
and bury them one more time,
drag a big bag to the cellar.
For a month their madness goes
unnoticed. Near Thanksgiving,
we switch on the light
and find them, hair in their eyes,
long pink tendrils groping
toward the window
dim with sun.

Ode to Steelhead

Hip-deep in the Salmon,
I scoop a handful
of gravel, finger
a tiny luminous globe
in my palm—an egg
the size of a small bead,
pink and glistening,
buried when the female
fluked up sand
and the male shot milt
for seed. Lifting it,
I see the eyes, black,
peering like probes.
I rebury it in the gravel
and remember: a smolt
becomes a sea-run trout,
a lunker bucking
lures and hope, lunging
the baffles from Bonneville
to Lower Granite,
nine hundred miles
to the headwaters of the Salmon,
its charred skin peeling
like last year's leaves,
news the eagles read
in Hells Canyon.

Palouse

There is always an empty house
by the road at the edge of town,
its windows whiskered with lilac
and letting in rain. Nearby,
a barn drags itself home,
and in May, daffodils trim the yard
against an ocean of wheat
that rolls in on a slow inexorable tide.

Passage

Jackpines jail the moon.
You take a flashlight
from the jockeybox, make
a pale swath through
the pasture. Quail skitter

into the black bloom
of gully-bordered fields.
The barn looms like a barrow.
Your light dances on the slats
like a swallow's ghost,

hovering, searching thatch.
Inside, the Morgan stamps in his stall.
Neither of us dreams
your belly burns with cancer,
that one more spring

will turn you back to fields.
The moon is rising.
We step out shivering in the light
and walk back toward the house
while quail in the hollows

usher in the night.

in memory of Dan Parker

Vanishing Point

East of Starbuck
the highway lies down
flat as a farmer's
best pressed Sunday tie.
At noon, wind weaves
a jet-trail through a maze
of powerlines west.
Ghost-funnels dance in the wheat.
After church, a farmer
tosses his tie out
through the car window.
The stalk it clings to
bends like a fiddlebow
and the wind keeps time
thumbing the pages of a bible
dropped on the gravel road.

Michael J. Kiefel

By the Sunshine You Ride

Old black man, pedalling now
   past the sage and soup cans
     of a vacant lot
you are brushed by the
   sunshine   you ride   the wind
     against   the wrinkles
of your brow   blowing the top of
   your head   clean off
     till your face is a baby's face
       except for the beard.

Did you find child's legs   somewhere
   back there   in the dump
     to pump you   so freely   against time
       when the newspapers rolling under you
   claim clearly   that you must be
       among the most miserable
       and depressed
     if you can even be at all?

You, dressed so splendidly in cords
   of muscle   move   with marble-smooth
     skin and bones   as though
your ragged clothes   serve as nothing more
   than dust-covers   to protect
       fine sculptory.

The artist who shaped you must have loved you
     too much
     to confine you   to a still life.

Every Shape that Carves a Color

You have daughters in the wind
     gathering bouquets of every shape that
       carves a color from the sky.

You paste an idea to a page
     as you would pin down a butterfly
       and call it a poem
       and pass it around at readings
       and everyone flutters wings.

But back there, back there
    the ground from which you plucked your concept
        by the roots
     and received the ransom of a little verse
   cries out of the hole you left,
      "The price you must pay for kidnapping
         is to stand in the place of what you stole,
        for what you take away
           must be answered for with your life."

There is an old woman on Maple street
   who has butterflies for ears.
She lets them fly off whenever they wish.
The roses in her cheeks have never wilted
     for she has never tried to transplant them
         into anyone else's plan for a landscape garden.
They say she burned her house down last year
        because she was frustrated with how her window sash
        tried to frame the sky.
I'm beginning to believe the story—
   I've never seen her anywhere but outside.
If you see her in your bushes or in the flower bed,
   keep still.
They say she has only six months to live.

Huckleberry Pilgrimage to Mount Thomas

Last of summer: cast of long shadows:
     woods burr with zimming yellow bees
     blurring nectar with sun as they burrow
   into drooping blossoms to tap
    a bit of the final sweetness.

We, too, attempting to storm Eden before the Fall,
     wade waist-deep among leaves that already
      have taken on the color of their fruit,
     burgundy-splashed even before the first frost.

Onward we stumble headlong, humbled by unseen holes,
    stagger among the bracken and crumpling tamarac till,
    from the road soon lost,
        we genuflect suddenly, unexpectedly,
            into proper kneeling positions for beholding
    these plump evening-colored berries
        which we will come to revere
    as much as any beads we might tell prayers upon.

Each berry, even when crowned by hot sap
    from the pine high above, carries the coolness
        of late August nights and the aura of lakes
            as they nestle changing stars.

We press them to our lips and remember
    what is always forgotten:
    that we always kiss much more than we can see.
Then we taste, overcome by temptation,
    and with shadow-blue tongues, we curse softly
    each time one of these hard-to-get gems escapes
        our stained fingers and rolls into the underbrush
    (which seems as utterly bottomless
    as the buckets we're trying to fill).

When, at the last tip of sunset, we have not yet
    filled pails and pouches and paunches,
    we surrender reluctantly and pack our
    tender living jewels
        back to a city where those who don't know
    mutter, "Blueberries are much sweeter,"
    and we, stained and gory veterans
        who could never tell the whole story,
savor how much of a mountain summer
        we'll never let sour in a huckleberry,
and we chew each one as carefully
    and as slowly
        as we'd picked it.

Linda Kittell

Bats

When my parents poured cocktails, I walked uptown
through the arch of pines, under the tall maples
that lined the Lockerby pasture, toward the Methodist Church.
Reverend Huddle let me practice on
the old pump organ, the one Sabra grunted at
Sunday after Sunday. I pedaled notes
on these summer evenings, played the simplest
inventions, left hand in awkward imitation
of right, the combination too often impossible. And often
I stayed to well past dark
until I knew my feet had to pedal
the oil-smoothed dirt toward home, too late
to miss the bats that played
their intricate patterns on the dark.
Their high squeals reminded me of black webs, the wings
that once a summer
made their way down our cottage chimney. Too often I remember
covering my head, my thongs flipping pebbles against my calves,
my feet searching their way down the alley
of maples, to pines, to the dark cedars
that edged our land until, in the distance,
I could hear my parents' laughter, the rhythmic clink
and tinkle of ice against glass, the sudden cadences
of my father's voice and could stop
a moment, brush the hair
off my forehead, straighten
my music and at last
catch my breath.
It's been a long time
since I've heard those island voices work
in tapestry, their laughter my protection
against a world of swirling motion, bats moving
into the night air.

Island Geography

In the fifth grade, Mrs. McKie
let us do maps of the island, spending
day after day with the slow process
of paint, plywood, salt and flour clay. I colored my board
aqua, the lake changed to the shade of seawater,
then shaped green clay into
the awkward oval of my island—the Head to the south,
the only bridge just northeast of Lighthouse Point.
I made orchards of twigs and popcorn, blushing the apple blossoms
pink with my sister's only nail polish. I painted
lollypop sticks into cattails, marking the marsh
that nearly cut
the island in half. Marble chips from the post office
filled my quarries, formed miniature gravestones on the way
to Monkey Hill. The Shrine was toothpicks, the Methodist Church
stiff matchsticks and more clay. I took one hotel
from the Monopoly set and five or six
of the green plastic houses—I needed two stores,
the garage and p.o., my house and LaFountains'.
We all left out the school until
Mrs. McKie brought in tiny matchboxes covered in red
construction paper, windows drawn in in marker. This
is my island, I thought. Wherever I looked
I saw a point of land I recognized: Jordan Point, Cloak Island,
The Sisters in the distance, mainlands to the east
and west, Alburgh Tongue north of us. In less
than a day, I could walk every road and say hello
to any person I could meet. This was home
and years later I can still feel the heft of it
resting on the palms of my hands.

Old Home Day

Always August hot, Old Home Day is
Mr. Carlson's excuse to get drunk and wave
from the seat of his son's
convertible. Grand Marshall of
the three-vehicle parade, he leads them past
the fire company and Nelson Beasley's pickup filled with relics
of taxidermy—a two-headed calf, the dusty
albino fawn that tips
over at the turns. At the Methodist Church
the kitchen steams with chicken pot pies, corn,
Sabra's rolls rising out of their pans and rows
of jello salads melting
into gravy.
                    Even the Catholics come, the farmboys—
Berger, Manzer and Junebug, the Vaschon brothers
in ironed coveralls and plaids, mopping the sweat,
waiting for the third sitting. Everything forms
a pool of wet: the tablecloths sweat, watermelon pickle
turns paler, meringue tears.
                              The dog with the road-dead toad floats
from the church to the orchard's shade. And every time
Rhonda LaBombard serves dessert,
we hold our breaths, wait
for the button on that white cotton blouse
to burst open
and cool the air.

Carolyn Kizer

A Poet's Household

Three for Theodore Roethke

The stout poet tiptoes
On the lawn. Surprisingly limber
In his thick sweater
Like a middle-aged burglar.
Is the young robin injured?

She bends to feed the geese
Revealing the neck's white curve
Below her coiled hair.
Her husband seems not to watch,
But she shimmers in his poem.

A hush is on the house,
The only noise, a fern
Rustling in a vase.
On the porch, the fierce poet
Is chanting words to himself.

By the Riverside

> *Do not call from memory—all numbers have changed.*
>
> From the cover of the
> telephone directory

Once I lived at a Riverside
1-3-7-5, by a real stream, Hangman's Creek,
Named from an old pine, down the hill
On which three Indians died. As a child,
I modeled the Crucifixion on that tree
Because I'd heard two Indians were thieves
Strung up by soldiers from Fort Wright in early days,
But no one remembered who the third one was.

Once, in winter, I saw an old Indian wade,
Breaking the thin ice with his thighs.
His squaw crouched modestly in the water,
But he stood up tall, buck-naked. "Cold!" he said,
Proud of his iron flesh, the color of rust.
He grinned as he spoke, struck his hard chest a blow
One, with his fist. . . . So I call, from memory,
That tall old Indian, standing in the water.

And I am not put off by an operator
Saying, "Sor-ree, the lion is busy. . . ."
Then, I would tremble, seeing a real lion
Trammeled in endless, golden coils of wire,
Pawing a switchboard in some mysterious
Central office, where animals ran the world,
As I knew they did. To the brave belonged the power.
Christ was a brave, beneath that gauzy clout.

I whispered to the corners of my room, where lions
Crowded at night, blotting the walls with shadows,
As the wind tore at a gutter beneath the eaves,
Moaned with the power of quiet animals
And the old pine, down the hill,
                              where Indians hung:
Telling my prayers, not on a pale-faced Sunday
Nor to a red God, who could walk on water
When winter hardened, and the ice grew stronger.

Now I call up god-head and manhood, both,
As they emerged for a child by the Riverside.
But they are all dead Indians now. They answer
Only to me. The numbers have not changed.

Persephone Pauses

The lengthened shadow of my hand
Holding a letter from a friend
Tells time: the sun descends again.
So long, so late the light has shone.
Since rising, we have shone with ease:
perhaps not happiness, but still
A certain comfort from the trees
Whose crests of leaves droop down in tiers,
Their warm trunks veiled by aspen hair,
Their honeyed limbs, the loosened earth
About the roots; while flowers recline
In dusty gardens, rest on weeds,
Those emblems of a passing year.

So be it! As I turn, my train
Is plucked by spikes of summer grass.
No clutch of summer holds me here.
I know, I know. I've gone before.
I glance to my accustomed glass,
The shallow pond, but films of slime
Waver across it, suck the verge
Where blunted marsh frond cuts the air.
But as I stare, the slime divides
Like curtains of old green velour:

I gaze into my gaze once more,
Still veiled in foam. But then, the grim
Tragedian from the other shore
Draws near my shade. Beneath the brim,
In motions formal and austere,

We circle, measure, heel to hem.
He proffers me an iron plate
Of seedy fruit, to match my mouth.

My form encased in some dark stuff
He has bedizened, keeps me hid
Save for that quivering oval, turned
Half-moon, away, away from him
And that excitement of his taste
He suffers, from my flesh withdrawn.

But this unwilling touch of lust
Has moved some gentle part of me
That sleeps in solstice, wakes to dream
Where streams of light and winter join.
He knows me then; I only know
A darkened cheek, a sidelong lower,
My nerves dissolving in the gleam
Of night's theatrical desire,
As always, when antagonists
Are cast into the sensual
Abysses, from a failing will.
This is my dolor, and my dower.

Come then, sweet Hell! I'll name you once
To stir the grasses, rock the pool,
And move the leaves before they fall.
I cast my letter to the breeze
Where paper wings will sprout, and bear
It on to that high messenger
Of sky, who lately dropped it here,
Reminding me, as I decline,
That half my life is spent in light.
I cast my spirit to the air,
But cast it. Summertime, goodnight!

Singing Aloud

We all have our faults. Mine is trying to write poems.
New scenery, someone I like, anything sets me off!
I hear my own voice going on, like a god or an oracle,
That cello-tone, intuition. That bell-note of wisdom!

And I can't get rid of the tempting tic of pentameter,
Of the urge to impose a form on what I don't understand,
Or that which I have to transform because it's too grim as it is.
But age is improving me: Now, when I finish a poem

I no longer rush out to impose it on friendly colleagues.
I climb through the park to the reservoir, peer down at my own
            reflection,
Shake a blossoming branch so I am covered with petals,
Each petal a metaphor. . . .

By the time we reach middle life, we've all been deserted and robbed.
But flowers and grass and animals keep me warm.
And I remind myself to become philosophic:
We are meant to be stripped down, to prepare us for something
            better.

And, often, I sing aloud. As I grow older
I give way to innocent folly more and more often.
The squirrels and rabbits chime in with inaudible voices.
I feel sure that the birds make an effort to be antiphonal.

When I go to the zoo, the primates and I, in communion,
Hoot at each other, or signal with earthy gestures.
We must move further out of town, we musical birds and animals,
Or they'll lock us up like the apes, and control us forever.

The Great Blue Heron

M.A.K., September, 1880-September, 1955

As I wandered on the beach
I saw the heron standing
Sunk in the tattered wings
He wore as a hunchback's coat.
Shadow without a shadow,
Hung on invisible wires
From the top of a canvas day,
What scissors cut him out?
Superimposed on a poster
Of summer by the strand
Of a long-decayed resort,
Poised in the dusty light
Some fifteen summers ago;
I wondered, an empty child,
"Heron, whose ghost are you?"

I stood on the beach alone,
In the sudden chill of the burned.
My thought raced up the path.
Pursuing it, I ran
To my mother in the house
And led her to the scene.
The spectral bird was gone.

But her quick eye saw him drifting
Over the highest pines
On vast, unmoving wings.
Could they be those ashen things,
So grounded, unwieldy, ragged,
A pair of broken arms
That were not made for flight?
In the middle of my loss
I realized she knew:
My mother knew what he was.

O great blue heron, now
That the summer house has burned
So many rockets ago,
So many smokes and fires
And beach-lights and water-glow
Reflecting pin-wheel and flare:
The old logs hauled away,
The pines and driftwood cleared
From that bare strip of shore
Where dozens of children play;
Now there is only you
Heavy upon my eye.
Why have you followed me here,
Heavy and far away?
You have stood there patiently
For fifteen summers and snows,
Denser than my repose,
Bleaker than any dream,
Waiting upon the day
When, like gray smoke, a vapor
Floating into the sky,
A handful of paper ashes,
My mother would drift away.

The Worms

Let Dodo rejoice with the purple worm. . . .
. . . the worm hath a part in our frame.
For I rejoice like a worm in the rain. . . .

                       Christopher Smart

This was childhood:
Walking through the worms
After a rain,
Trying not to wound
Anything alive;
Most especially
Not to maim the self
By any kind of death.

Move among the worms,
Pearly and purple,
Curling and opal,
Tickled by the sidewalk,
Heaped over the lines
Of childhood's first map:
Step on a line
Break your mother's spine,
Step on a crack
Break your mother's back.

Take care of mother,
Beware of father,
Protect foot and finger,
My heart and my heel.
Tiptoe on the spaces,
Don't tread on sex!

Like in small forms—
Hop-toads, lobelia,
Moreover, worms,
The recently born—
Whelms us in childhood:
We grow as we move
Close to the ground,
Eyes in our toes.

Crumbling, cool
And many-dimensioned,
The morsels of soil
Cling to a worm
When he comes to rain
Fresh from the ground:
Bruised as a blueberry,
Bare as a rose,
Vulnerable as veins,
Naked as a nose.
The earth-worm smell
Of each commencement,
The sense that the new
Owns all that it is.
When the torrents end,
God gloats at the world.

Judith Kleck

Crows

Sun transcribes
the berry vines
as morning wakes

beyond this window
where some small
measure of hope,

finds one crow
a piece of bread,
carries it to
the warming road.

Another, close by,
hops over.
Another flies
down.

Two more appear,
drop from branches
like dead weight.

There is no
struggle here
but the gawk
and squawk and

casual insistence
of those who must scrounge
a living each

and every day,
counting less on the crumbs
of kindness than the
thoughtless casting away.

Impromptu for Sarn

All morning at the piano
I think of nothing but
the uncontrollable notes
breaking out of reach.

Outside my neighbor whistles,
improvising a garden beyond the steps
near the backyard fence

where last summer's scraps of leaves
and vines remind me that Beethoven's *Adieu*
pays homage to such things.

I have grown a garden with awkward hands,
thinned cabbages, tossed an unruly carrot
to the garbage bin and felt in each
the weight of the smallest loss,
the slightest sound.

Between each measure I remember my son
given to his father, how each note
has its own distinction, that music
requires attention to time—

I am forgiven in those moments when music
becomes music and nothing is played:
when I move as pure, transparent form,
abstract as the thumb's mute motion
towards the hand's correctness.

Turning Stones

for Joe

I refuse to count days
hearing a marriage that lasted seven years
would last forever. Now beneath the bridge

I used to cross, wanting a way out,
or in again, we've stopped to turn stones,
searching for an agate this valley
and Tibet provide. We refuse
to undo this puzzle, roughly exotic,
return each rock to its familiar place.

Blue one, blue one. My words weave
the grasses leaning with the river.

Evenings we mark time by the pages
turned and I imagine we read the same words,
in different orders, taking separate languages
to a common bed: your reticence undone
by the body's stark commitment,
your shoulders knotted as the rocks
I turned in my hand.

Blue one, blue one. Your love's a stone
I take, I give back again.

Widower

Somewhere it ended, as always,
without ceremony. Summer,
the lust-bound season, spent
in its own heat.

Where was I when it slipped by
like the death of a friend of a friend,
like all the deaths I read of here,
daily & anonymous?
Up from the tangle of shrubs, juncos
in cocky black flyer's caps
now scatter the seeds and bother
the rosy finches into retreat.

The day advances full of birds
and their relentless advances, retreats.
Next door the widower's woodpile
blocks his view of the river.
He's lit an early fire;
smoke shifts into the trees

and words no longer belong,
like summer or birds, to what they once
defined. Yet the images linger,
the mourning they rely on.
The first cold wind is down
from the mountains where the season
has long since turned, pushing
the deer before it, forcing
a winter song: *names be with us.*
Wind, grieve gently over our head.

Alex Kuo

A Chinaman's Chance

Shanghai, *1945*

When the bombs dropped on us at the end of the war
No one knew which side did it. We were under
Blankets, beds, that inside table, even chairs

Later when I walked out of the dropzone, I counted
The steps that were not mapped at the beginning
Wanting everyone to have the same, necessary things

Hundreds were queued up on every street corner
For airdropped powdered milk, chocolate, condoms
By the same planes that dropped the bombs the night before

If the truth be known, I had to kill to get away
Lucky, as luck would have it, I wasn't born
In the 18th century: Mozart loved slurs then

For heroes now, I retain Clemente, Gould, my two sons
And what the wind leaves: they have been here
All this time nearer my life, nearer my starfield

For direction, I call on the far points
That insist at intervals without explanation
That left with me in the last, unmarked C-46

Like that last flight out of Casablanca in 1940
In the fog and at gunpoint, just like that
Shutting out of a life, leaping out past the finish

Do not mistake me or look for me in another meaning
Where I won't be found. In a sense we have all survived
Our words depend on it, with each chance

A Rose by any Other Name

On this day that I think of her
40 yrs later from Moscow ID

I sketch a plant on my display screen
the only metaphor we have in common

the rose that belonged to her
Sweetbrier, Penzance, Fruehling's Gold

114

Cabbage, Frau Dagmar Hartopp, Fräulein
Ilse Koch, the Bitch Queen of Buchenwald

from her rose garden, nursed from the face
of season, all spring to fall

the spectacular cremations oh
how she watched the temperatures climbing

& the people waiting in line
& standing in mud, where skin turns to petal

peeling layer after layer
in the oven whorling like blown bookpages

bursting from their corners
& exploding into combustion

from human skin draped over lampframes
collecting dust the broom never touched

flickering from light to dark to flame
to Ash Bitch of Buchenwald

like rose corsages that are metaphor
that are she & me & you

which Sappho called *Queen* & now
fucked at last in greenhouses at $75 a doz

that I know enough, the stench of it
the flower that ends in ash

& not pressed in dictionaries, so don't talk
to me of how it's love or feels furry

where in Moscow wreathed in every living moment
the rose is that rose from that rose garden

is Ilse, is burning flesh, is all of us
the Bitch of Buchenwald.

from The Picture

The difference between what belongs and what doesn't
is the ability to balance between plateau and surf.
                                              —*L. Sebring*

Before daylight I am eager for rain. In my half-sleep the stream fills with furious birds. There is no electricity to speak of, so the water flows from top left to bottom right. There are no waves. By six swimmers exhaust the beach. Someone looks up and takes notes. With each new sentence something is repeated, some color restored, something unseen stirs between plateau and surf.

A figure steps out to the edge. She is taking a chance considering how exaggerated she looks.

A figure steps out to the edge. She is taking a chance, considering she might be a fugitive hiding from the camera since childhood.

Everything in the center is caught in someone's eye in the same quantity. The light behind me cannot escape, though the space between us depends on how far I am willing to walk. How easily I forget that there is no trail to the vertical except the one I forgive. In daylight it is every mapmaker's relief. The lines turn outward and balance against legend. What belongs and what doesn't is the difference in elevation.

Away from the children and the picnickers, the figure at the edge has not moved. What belongs here and what doesn't is a difference in seeing. Love me, love me, in this interval waiting. The space between us dips, and I lean over to her side at just the right moment and take her by the nipple. Anything is possible, she says. Our collusion thickens and branches to blood. The heart fills quickly, leaving no necessity for metaphor. Only the wind arches, and what it brings has not ceased since it began.

*

Sometimes I look down there and watch it going back in, retaining as much as possible. It is all here, without fiction and without question. There is no pause to name it.

Sheltering the Same Needs

this late in our century
a hot meal, warm clothes
someplace to sleep, is all

so many crammed into already-
crammed housing with Aunt Jo

lives edged-out by downtown
gentrification, someone always there
counting the rising index points

pretty soon they wear out their
welcome and are out on the streets

selling the Christmas tree
won in a Salvation Army drawing
"I don't feel it anymore"

eviction has replaced fire
as the most direct cause of homelessness

except maybe some brother-and-sister pair
whose background is hazy
no roots archived in anyone's photo

UNDELIVERABLE MAILS
DEAD LETTER BRANCH
PCC-390 MAIN STREET ROOM 354
S.F. CA. 94105-9502

eyes always glossed bitter with
astonishment, remembering the body
we resemble most, call nothing ours

the Cellophane Lady lived and died
just one block from her daughter's apartment

"they can do anything to me"
our one prayer, improbable in the nearest
quarter-mile, killing us with all we've got

The River

We live by it, bank deep
By choice near where some ducks
Have also come to believe
This fierce geography that the wind
Will not forget in the next change.

We live in it, in its echo
That is a question, and what it asks
Is a breath forming its words
There on the opposite century, here
On this seamless shore, this abundance.

One year I followed it back
To its beginning in a glacial gap
The next night all the seasons moved
A half moon over my head rising
At last released from all counting.

We live for it, in its story
Dispersed as we are flesh in its eddies
Of meaning, this wider water
And its settlement among leaves
Glittering with teeming assertion.

We live like this, our breath
Over the river's edge, reason
Collecting at the changing waterline
Where only a vague mark forms
Between promise and possibility.

Laurie J. Lamon

Returning

This the house, the lawn
where I am holding my sister's hand,
where I am the youngest.
We are standing up in the pool.
You are smiling, your free hand touching
my brilliant shirt of water.

The house, after all, is white.
I drive past the globes
of light, the voices I imagine
separately as the strands of a screen.

At the end of the street
the sun drops behind the Kaiser's backyard
twenty-five years ago,
the outline of trees where I walked in
and was lost, a forest
touching ground. The path now
is useless, coming out the other side.

Returning,
I recognize other children
by the pool, their mothers' fear of enclosure.
I imagine I am older.
Someone's voice
announces my arrival, my desire to leave.

Second Lives

Any longer it is useless to look up
into the rimmed trees,
your body stripped and shining
like money. Soon you will come home,
bringing all you wanted to say.
You will pull your chair into the room
and smoke, long after
the filling and passing of plates,
late into evening after the voice
calling through airless tunnels of leaves
returns whatever word
is missing. The hills fasten down.
Animals sink into the dark,
the moon pressed to their screened bodies.

Early and late
you sit down to this hour
weightless as the paper boats
that drifted farther each night
across the lake. The shore's murmur
where you woke between your mother, your father,
meant nothing: it was the sky
rising above itself and the lake,
the drowned oars floating out.

You understand we must find you.
Your wife arranges your suits on the bed.
Your absence gathers
the luster of mirrors, sits down
on the bright lawn.
You understand it is years
since you stopped beside the road
and walked in toward the lake, for once
the sky burdenless, the ground pointing away
from yourself and the losses
buried one by one like confessions
you dreamed you invented for this.
You walk in. The trees are on fire, the water already faithless and shining.

Situs

i.

You write you are memorizing
the names of birds, their soft gray bodies
spilling like shade
at noon into the courtyard.
You are always alone:
it's the way I imagine you, disappearing
beneath the surf, or in the open,
your flesh remembering the blue waves.

You send photos of birds, seals.
The dead ones float, you say, into clear pools.
A month goes by, a year.
You describe the wharf
and the calm boats going by,
the fixed bare faces.
Each morning you arrive early on the beach—
you keep digging,
bringing up more clams, more pink shells.
You send necklaces of light.

ii.

Moonlight floats above the coffee table.
Each room sinks into quietness.
I leave the house,
and the yard's promontory pushes off
from the lake.
Above me, the black pines,
a few stars.
The night shines soundless
as the acres of dark beyond the waves
and the fishing lights,
beyond my first memory of land left behind
at Coos Bay, the thin strip going white
and the sea coming up
without edges.

I can hear them,
the waves grinding softly in the other world
where you are waking, just now,
into that sunlight
you believe keeps the right distance
between us.

Eleanor Limmer

Celebration of a Storm

Dark clouds amass and spiral upward
in a hot summer sky.
There is a slow stirring of the wind
and the great trees shiver.
The waves clap an incessant beat against the shore,
and within the house I hear
doors of the houses slamming shut,
rain pelting the hot sidewalks.

Behind doors and windows,
people wait for what is heavy and held
to be born. The sweet smell of moist earth
rises like steam from a volcano vent.

Then a silver vein strikes the dark sky.
The lake is illuminated with a light
so intense, its image remains
an afterbirth, an umbilical cord,
silvered upon the retina.

Again and again
electric rivers, chains and veins
expose the lake
and the silhouettes of trees
battered and wild,
whipped and frenzied by the wind.

Behind their windows,
those who belong to the storm
dance along the luminous currents.
They resonate to the rumble
of giant barrels rolling down the hills.
Silvered volts
scintillate through their veins
and along their nerves.
An ancient excitement
is born into their expectant world.

Liberty

You shall know the truth and
the truth shall set you free.

There is no shadow of turning
in the eye of the osprey
when the truth of what he seeks
becomes one with him
when he dives
plummeting beak
and brown feathers plunging after
down the sky.

Then the silver truth he seeks
quivers there within his talons
alive and dripping
above the surface of the lake.
What was always there beyond
common sight is caught and held
up against the sky.

Dawn hits the sky
with a burst of orange blue light
scattering bright stars across the lake
and into the shadows of the houses
where the sleepers awaken,
one by one.

What each one looks upon,
he becomes. Some choose to be
a clear blue lake filled with stars
with clear blue minds
who see the morning stars
scatter their light across the lake
and grasp the blue wind beyond their fingertips.

Spokane Falls in Springtime

The river erupts
pouring its choked and glutted streams
into the central corridor of the solid city.

Under the closed eyes of the Water Power Building,
the river is crowded between cement and rock walls
into the spillway

where it is the light green color of new leaves
that have just burst
through their sticky winter casements.

It rolls over
like a fat woman
turning in her bed.

Then it leaps
with the paws of a hundred lions
and lands with froth between its teeth.

The lions fight
to climb back up
out of the cage of their lost freedom.

They hurl
themselves upon the rocks below
in a white rage of high mists and spattering steam.

The city turns in its business
unaware of the roar and hiss
coming from its center.
The white hiss
and roar of the water
stills and hushes below the bridges.

Even the pigeons seem unconcerned
with the green dream of a city
asleep in its sidewalks.

James J. McAuley

Drought

The phone sits on the wall, a starved insect.
I could call you anywhere on the globe,
It's me, Jim—chewed into thin whining strips
Of wire and wind and spittle. Nine hours sooner
Or later you'd choke down a tinny capsule
Of sound, don't you remember? *It's me, it's me!*
My hand unfolds from the phone, a stricken insect.

This is no occasion for a letter,
Except I have forgiven myself in time
For the dead I didn't write to. The seasons here
Effect so little change that when the lake
At Coeur d'Alene is lowest in memory,
It's surely worth my mentioning. Besides,
You can easily find that lake on any globe,

Even so small a scale; and it's close to where
I live. All through these parts the drought gains ground.
Our neighbours, who at the best of times are silent,
Now are fervidly dumb. Good luck is the thin
Stalk in the flowerpatch that held the head
Of the pale aster for a week, then let go.
You could be dead, and I would still write this letter.

Letter to Richard Hugo from Drumcliff

Dear Dick, This kind of travel is cheap enough:
Hard a'starboard after a vexing nightmare,
And there I leave you—Mister Yeats at Coole
Being severe with young poets on Lady Gregory's lawn,
Looking over his specs at a few bedraggled sheep
On the shore of the murky lake. And he counting them swans....

It's just a Byzantine canter through Roscommon,
A fearful county for tinkers, to Drumcliff.
A Philip Larkin chapel, half-buried in old trees;
Bland, tame Gothic of the Established Faith
That none of the neighbours give a damn about,
Keeping to their long-lipped superstitions,
Their guttural gossip making a natural prey
Of the ancestral rector—"He's a nice man, *but*...."
Half-starved mongrels worrying a lame sheep.

125

The embattled cleric: patrolling his neat grounds,
Pondering his fingernails, the only
Clean set in the parish; preparing to preach mildly
On "Prudence" again, to his congregation of five—
Six, if you counted the deafmute poorhouse orphan,
His only convert, who rang the Communion bell
And pulled the thistles from the gentry's graves.

The peasantry: He sang them plain and cruel,
Dour and quaint; went sour on them, invented
A freckled ghost in tweed with a fly-rod and an ear
Cold enough to hear him out. He caught
Neither salmon nor trout himself; hated low bars;
His women all had double-barrelled names.
How could *we* move in *his* circles? His goddam gyres!

Randy laughter, hell! His lightest rhyme
Was strictly Big House—a bronze gong embossed
With gyres, moon-phases, rose, rood, and tower;
Struck well, that great gong calls the lords and ladies
To their places at stage centre, *right.* He warped
The local colours of old saga, older *rann,*
To his own passionate, visionary weft,
As Vergil had for Rome in *her* decline.
Here, beneath white gravel, his immortal, bone-white grin.

There's an old cross at the top of the graveyard lane.
The disproportionate head of the crucified figure
Wears the same dissembling agony-smile.
Some nameless monk, ten centuries ago,
Chipped the lichen off a great rock and cut
Him down to size.
So, that gorgeous gong resounds through Idaho:
Here, the tourist looks up from the arrogant plain stone
To a rook flapping in a galebent oak. It's like
Getting pissed off at Xerxes, as you say. Best, Jim.

Pool at the Y

Lawyers and salesmen muscled around
Naked in the locker room, restive as sharks.

They rubbed and shrugged under the showers.
Pink or tanned, paunched or lean, they stood

As one kind with him, lashing themselves
With water, or drooping under the jets,
steaming like beasts of burden.

*

Light from high overhead swayed
On empty green water. After a boy

Jack-knifed from the low board, he eased
Into the flashing rippling, and was changed.

A girl with nothing to hide in her lycra skinsuit
Sprawled in her chair and vaguely smiled.

In a space vaulted like this, Virgins and Martyrs
Fostered the right ways of life and death,
Back in the age of sin.

*

But here was the Age of Vigor. He pushed off
And thrashed out a length. Then back.

Chlorine scoured his eyes. He slowed and rolled
Down a green cheering universe, and back,

Stroke by stroke, shouldering the invisible
Rope of water, until he tired and climbed out.

The lovely lifeguard smiled upon water and light
Admiringly, and on him. But she stayed to keep watch

Over the other swimmers while the sauna's heat
Took him by the scalp and led him down
A single step, into the Age of Age.

Running in Snow

From the roadside the undersides
Of boughs and cornices blacken
To my liking. The sky drifts
My way, and melts on my lip.

Ache, ache, little bird,
Hiding under my shoulder.

Where have my footsteps gone?
A mile or more slipped away
Since I heard their steady tapping
Lead me through the hush.

Snow has filled each step.
Yet a dark track pulses
Just out of sight. A pheasant
Mocks from a whitening field.

Steady, steady, bird
Twittering in my throat.

The void spins round behind,
Above; draws me upwind of silence.
Particle by particle, the world
Blindly remakes itself.

Quiet, quiet, bird
Hopping on the ridge of my spine.

High Drive whirls into a silvery nothing.
Hangman Valley's a muffled rumor.
A car passes, quiet as cancer;
One headlight eats into the sky.

Houses gather in their streets
Like museum displays. Traffic
Thickens, murmuring through
Swirling veils, dead slow.

Sing, sing little bird
In your cage under my shoulder.

Mansions, domes, cathedrals
Appear and dissolve. I have come
Through our galaxy, atom by atom:
My home could be anywhere.

Sing, sing, little bird.

Spokane Perspective

for Carolyn Kizer

For blocks the derelicts
Drop back behind one another,
Glass gone from the windows,
To a billboard by the freeway.
Beyond that, the pines on a cliff
Are poised like a green *tsunami.*

The scene requires no motion,
But the pigeons fidget anyway
On the parapet of a warehouse
Dolled up as a Renaissance villa
Powdered with dust blown in
From wheatfields behind the rimrock.

Developers ransacked history
For that *decor*—Gothic France,
The Moors, Tudor England—to furnish
Their Inland Empire with streets
Fit for boosters and go-getters.

The lights change one after the other
The length of the half-empty street:
Red to green, red to green, red to green,
Retreats like a disappointed
Salesman from Chicago.

Not a building in view where anyone
Takes calls from a desk awash
In paper, or scolds a subordinate,
Or pauses at a window
To regard the restive pigeons.

Look out beyond the freeway: don't you want
Those pines to sweep down over the whole damned city?

The Exile, *En Famille*

Among my own, I'm a figure of fun,
A bare-fanged clown, even in anger.
When I'm half-asleep over a book
Of literary criticism, or consumed
By passions that last a week for eating apples
Or gluing models or pruning plum-trees—in
My clumsiness, untidiness, my untimely
Trade, my distractedness, they mock
Generously. I've learned to pay them
No mind. Without contempt, my children
Ignore my commands, my rules for safety first,
Tuning their nerves to a frequency
That transmits but won't receive.
But that's all right: for their part,
They burden me with tasks so trivial,
Oiling a hinge, fixing a window, tying
A shoelace, while my head is filled
With keeping a ketch's bow into the wind,
Or listening to Brahms and Tolstoy talking
While they stroll a riverbank—I accomplish
Their love at small cost. As the trout
Leaping from the pool in the willow shade
Needs the deadly air to remind him
Of his element, and would not forego
The glistening arch he carves—
So, while I bend to repair
The broken window, I remember:
I accomplish their love at small cost.

Ron McFarland

Connecting Flights

In the darkened car
at the far end of the runway
the farmer's daughter
stares into the night sky
dreaming of San Diego.
Behind her the windbreak pines,
black against the clouds,
tell where her father's wheat
begins or where their house
breaks the horizon.
These turboprops go
nowhere of consequence.
They barely make it in and out
much of the year,
high-class cropdusters,
small potatoes blown off-course,
updrafted, junior pilots
jockeying for jet jobs,
working their way up
from the ground.
And she has seen the ground
close up, fingernail and knuckle,
crosswind dust
choking her last thought
short of getting out.
Now Eddie sits beside her
thinking God knows what,
his touch
stiff on her bare shoulder,
thinking dark green
winter wheat
half under the late spring snow
thawing, growing all night,
the next day, all summer,
harvest, the next sowing.
The farmer's daughter stares
hard over dark hills
to catch the red flicker
of landing lights, a small
airplane going somewhere,
anywhere at all.

Idaho Chain Saw Massacre

Some poor schnook like you slays himself
each year trying to save himself a few bucks
on firewood, hacking tamarack and white pine
out of the near wilderness in sheer delight
of noise, metallic wracking of the woods
worse than a million magpies, trail bikes,
ravens cracking the air with their squawks.

They draw themselves from warm homes,
love, gardens plump with late tomatoes.
Out in the haunted woods the trees have fallen
over themselves in criss-cross heaps.
These are rotten, dank with decay.
But the tallest trees may be the deadliest.
A snag suddenly snaps at your chain saw,
clips you in a vicious embrace
without saying a word. Just "swish,"
faster than air can carry the sound
to your ear, and before you can know it
you are broken everywhere and your blood
creeps into the blackness fresh and unseen.
Or some poor devil yanks the starter cord,
only to turn away at the wrong moment
thinking he heard a bear or cougar
tearing the brush to maul him for dinner.
Then what a surprise your saw has in store
for the flesh and bone of your leg!
Shock alone protects you from the pain
that's killing you while you think you're
crawling back to your pick-up, and your mind
cooperates. It sees you at Rusty's Tavern
telling of the mean steel kiss your chain saw
inflicted just above your knee and how,
pouring just one last red beer,
it made you hold your breath forever.

Man's Death Mars Race

Hundreds rush past the lilac bushes
where his long legs have crumpled
like a crushed paper cup, discarded,
and he tries to clutch his heart two-handed
where it jabs under the flesh and bony ribs
exploding under the heavy aroma, and he thinks,
exhaling the dense fragrance, damn
now he'll have to limp into the back of the pack
and start all over as soon as these
flashing apologetic feet breeze past.

And how embarrassing this is to slip
into this painfully awkward heap
before hardly getting started, and how his wife
will tease about his receding hair. But the pain
striding across his threshold
takes his mind off her foolishness, and the thick
sweet odor of lilac reminds him it's time to rise
right now and join the fun and not
ruin it for everyone before the sun
lowers its warm black curtain.

The Worley Club Cafe

The highway bends just right for a place like this,
slowing you straight into a gravelled parking space
and scrambled eggs folded like a formal handkerchief,
hashbrowns a flat rectangle, great coffee.
You thought this place was famous for something,
not eggs, God knows. They're out of pie today.

Everyone here has a first name but you.
The waitress could be your grandmother, the one who
refused to go to your parents' wedding, cut you
out of her will, and left it all to the Humane Society.

The guy at the counter drives a hard bargain
on his hard-driven pickup etched a faded blue
against the wheat stubble. He'll throw in the pair
of stuffed pink dice he won at the fair, and the gun rack
but not the rifle. The short order cook is hooked.

After ten this place gets back to normal,
just the waitress saying this is her last cup,
the cook washing up and hauling into the mountains
in his faded blue dream, the giant moosehead
under which you ate so fearlessly glowering steady
through his bright glass eyes, and you driving away.

Why You Think You're in Idaho

Maybe you think you came to beat the high price
of city life, or to raise your kids
sensibly, the way you were not brought up.
Maybe you think anything is better than
Nebraska, Iowa, the flat Midwest,
or the poured cement of California,
or the boredom of your first life,
the anguish of a mad marriage,
booze, a few bad years in college.
You find yourself not knowing where to go,
so you think it may as well be Idaho.

Maybe you think you came for the big game,
herds of elk or shoals of salmon
throwing themselves like living trophies
at your cold feet. Or maybe you think their
blood should not be spilled on your account.
You'll be content with long trails hiking
into the thin, pure air of the Bitterroots
or wandering aimless in the desert
west of Blackfoot, north of Burley,
anywhere from Arco. Sage grouse,
bear, jackrabbit, coyote, magpie,
you've thought of them all as you
relived the cold adventures of Lewis and Clark
or dreamed of Zion at Fort Lemhi,
wakening suddenly to the screams
of Shoshones, Bannocks, and Mormons.
On the Union Pacific line, you were Chinese.
In that case, think twice if you please.

Maybe you think you came to make your fortune
panning the panned-out streams for gold,
or mining the mountains for silver
at thirty dollars an ounce, or plowing
sugar beets or hard red winter wheat
at five dollars a bushel on a thousand acres
of land your grandparents won from long
winters, Indians, stones, and drought.
You'd better think again if you're in doubt.

Maybe you woke up one day and found yourself
here for no clear purpose whatever.
Rainbow trout leave you as cold as January.
Boston is all there is of history,
culture stops at the Mississippi,
resuming briefly at the Golden Gate, and you hate
farming with a passion. Even the trees
mean nothing in particular to you,
and you have neither friends nor relatives.
For being here you can have no ulterior motives.

James McKean

Bull Slaughter

All summer they have praised him
with sugar beets and hay,
given ground where he wanted ground,
water in his concrete trough,
silence and clear, cold mornings
he could fill with bellowing
and his breath drifting
shoulder-high over the fields.
But this morning the woman who fills
his trough stands far away,
hushing her children,
and behind her the man
who brings him sugar beets
kicks at nothing on the ground.
Other men in boots and aprons
watch him so intently that
all of his skin shudders.
They keep the distance he allows them
even now as they clap once
and his knees buckle,
even now as their hands cross
over and over the grinding steel,
even now as they bend down
and bless him with their sharpest knives.

Solstice

1. Summer

Sometimes thought dries up
like the stream beside my house
in the dead of summer
when the bed stones remember
what it was to expand.
Take, for instance, my rattling ice
in a glass and drawing
one cube across my forehead
and throwing it—a lazy
sidearm into this day full of heat,
full of my neighbor's clapping
her slippers to wake all dust,
full of hummingbirds
rifling her trumpet flowers,
full of sparrows beneath my feeder,
bathing in the soft dirt
at the far side of my yard
where the ice in its perfectly
dying arc lames one
in the wing. I couldn't have
hit it if I'd tried
or felt anything like I feel now,
walking barelegged in thorns
where the sparrow has lost itself,
where I find nothing to heal
but something bedded
in a hard place, beneath thought,
perfection its final aim.

2. Winter

This morning the moon
sets so close the tallest branch
of my crab apple tree passes
behind it. Out my window
I see my neighbor late again,
hurrying in the dark
to fill his arms with firewood.
The robins, at work already,
clip the crab apples from my tree.
I think it measures only itself
all year: red blossoms dropping
no farther than the reach
of its farthest branch, then leaves,
now crab apples lost in the snow.
I have waited another year
for the sun to rise
no farther south than ever.
I have waited for the beauty
and sadness of this like a child
who backs into his father's door,
one hand flat on his head,
knowing he has grown no taller,
or the robins that leave
in their search the bare snow outline
of the branches of my tree,
or my neighbor who drives to work at last,
one of his taillights out,
one bright like a small, bitter apple
found in the snow.

Stump Farm

for my brother

A crop in perpetual failure
you say, laughing all day beneath a sky
gray as hardpan. We've cut firewood
until my truck groans in its springs,
and now we sit and drink and watch the sky
darken as a bruise darkens, the stumps
gone black on your two muddy acres—
a good idea you thought
until your wife left at night, the wolf
wild in her veins, her headlights
crazy in the trees that fall now
one by one around you. Stump farm—
pasture someday, a good fence,
maybe a single-wide towed in, blocked up,
and water if the pipes don't freeze.
She left what she couldn't move:
the garage you sleep in, your gift horse
that bit her once too often, bruises
rising in her arms like two-petalled flowers,
even your dumb anger no one sees,
that holds the riding crop at your side
when the horse swings backside out,
steel shoes flashing. It's as if
you can't break something inside you
stubborn as stumps that will not budge
come prybar or peavy or weeks of fire,
come desperate late-night seedings of mud
for pasture rising green and even
come spring, come spring.

The Desert

The easiest thing to do here is build a road.
    A cow looking for water will,
But more often than not find nothing but itself
    Crazed on jimsonweed, stock-still,
Sore-bellied, trying to drink up the sand.
And its persistent neighbors—the Swainson's hawk, the crow—
All the harbingers of disaster wait for the end,
    The last cry that shakes the bitterbrush,
        When a few survive
By cleaning the bones of those who travel here and
    End where they arrive.

Yet it is curious how most things adjust:
    The winterfat, the thyme buckwheat
Leaning away from the sand-filled wind, or sagebrush
    Closing down in the midday heat.
And after a meeting of cautious eyes
How the darkling beetle yields to the grasshopper mouse
To the desert night snake to, at last, the burrowing owl—
    This marriage of victim and victor
        With its deadly union
Consummated between the falling sun and the rise
    Of a frozen moon.

Even I may live by turning the earth upside down,
    Piling sand around me for walls.
I wait like a seed underground, then rise each
    Morning to walk the dry rills,
To hunt the black-tailed hare, the sage grouse,
And return before the sun explodes. Some days the air
Will promise rain, and as I watch a few clouds blacken,
    The desert blooms, the sand turning green in
        A moment's shower.
Time to bathe before the sun returns. What blooms
    Will die in an hour.

There's a Hawk in the Yard

Pale, as tall as the thumb
at the length of my arm
before the tallest tree, a hawk
stalls, found out, skulking,
now sparrows riot in the poplars,
now enterprise stops,
now the day brightens with fear
and noise, the wind having brought us
danger—there's a hawk in our yard,
preceded by his shadow
so we all knew of his coming,
so we all pay his tax of attention, eyes
forward, breath steady
in honor of what's in store someday
when we're not looking or fat
with supper or sick but not dead, just
our wakefulness gone, and
we find ourselves fleeing, winded
and slow, out into the open.
This is called revelation and giving
for which the hawk loves us all
one day and stoops, wings folded in adoration
of what it will enter talons first,
of what will sustain him.
But not today. Let him hop around
for locusts, dusty and awkward, found out
and a failure, wind-rumpled for
sitting so still above us, our fool
until he flies away.

James R. McLeod

Archetypes

What does it matter
what the mind's
own pattern is?
Each varies its cold edge
as the icy etch of flake.
But at our root
salmon swell mad as rivers,
leave the nerves
raw as a sliced eel
to sing as deep
as Achilles' grief.

What does it matter
that the ink-shocks
remind us we are blind
to the same tree?
Or how behind the eye's stare,
light goes as silverfish
in old bindings?
Know only that the same rain
will silt our bones
after the archetypes fail.

Drowning with Brock

If only, my son,
saving were as easy
as that day on the docks
when you were three.
While I labored
at the engine's head,
you flailed
at the boat's bow
until a sound
at the edge of mind
as hackled as a wolf's fear
whined above the drill's dull pitch.

142

I moved, then, as quick
as a snake's eye
to see
your face obscuring
as the moon
in November cloud.
Your taut hand
stretched
at the long surface,
then mine,
breaking that wet pulse,
drawing you out,
like that surgeon
armed in blood
from your mother, breech.
Then, for an instant,
you froze
pale as clay,
fixed upon your feet,
until your terror
ebbed in tears,
and you clung to me
as tight as a melon's skin.
Now, years later,
I wake, in mid-dream,
shaking at my own surface,
and think
how long distant Alaska is,
and how
when we speak
our reaching's obscured
as time's stopped mouth,
and how, in the dark,
I still hear you call me
father.

Making the Arrows

First we find the flint
buried near your pup's bones
far from your mother's garden.
Years ago,
when the moon split standing stones,
as if to explain
crescent and change,
stone could be shaped
by a sudden blow
calibrated in the skull.
Painted bison
on the cave roof
bore their scars.

Now we shatter stone upon stone,
search for substantial points
knowing how the finding
and the tying
reflect what's broken
and what's of use.

If only this bound flint,
would fly as true
as this moment, my son.
If only arrows believed in time
and the wounds they make,
they could help us find
how to live
when our distance
is longer
than your bow shot.

Now you must believe,
even, if summer's gone,
I've still stones
stored in my trunk.
Some nights
I strike them
in the dark
and pretend
the bison still live.

Saying Goodbye

This is no poem
touching your life
only the passing
of something like wind
between us.

Somewhere,
years from now,
that photo of your father's face
will seem fresh
as that sense
of what we have
and what we've left.

Some night
the sound of rain,
or a dog
in a distant shed,
will remind us
of ways
we've failed,
our grief larger than sky,
the same obsession
with misery in wind.
We'll remember
how we've let go
of what might have helped
and hung on
to what we'll surely lose.

Fran Polek

Similkameen Poems

1. River of Gold

Grey-broad, white-dappled, winter-cold,
curled between orange-faded general store
and abandoned hotel, near Big Chopaka's green-
frosted mountain pyramid frame—river of
our lust. Oh, Similkameen, Similkameen,
we chant your name, treasure bearer,
spawned on pre-historic Trepanege Plateau,
high British Columbia grail, cause of
constant hope. Water vault of high assayed
placer gold, we've yearned for you from
warm winter Spokane rooms, talked and
dreamed of you, imagined you gathering
your perdurable riches in the vastness
north of Princeton, slipping past Hedley,
Cawston and Richter Pass, burbling across
the border into our American grasp,
trilling over cold gravel bars, holding
tight your black sand secret, waiting for us.
We can make you happy, sweet Similkameen!

2. Discussion of Tactics
"Nope, don't think you fellers will find
anything up here. Why, two, three summers
ago, some big flushers with mountain-sized
dredge stayed all summer, got nothing,
no sir, got nothing."
We sit together in old wooden chairs in the
small store, watching the Similkameen roll
southward out the dirty windows. What does
he know?, we imagine. Why would the Seattle
group tell him what they found? Why was the
section available for our claim? We've
seen the Assay, our rights are filed in Olympia
on this bearing stretch of the river. They
sit and squint at us, wondering what they've
missed. "No sir," he says, the rancher from
near the border, "this river here, she's a
real bitch, a lousy rock carrier, a flooder,
a wanderer." *Beautiful,* we think, sipping our
coffee in cracked plastic mugs, *beautiful—*
perfect description of gold bearing water!
"You fellers going to put a dredge in the
water?" Maybe, we lie, maybe we'll pan a bit
here and there, for fun you know. "Oh Yeh,
we know," he said, "we've seen lots of you
on the Similkameen."

3. The Dredge
Some look at it and laugh, or joke
about raping the river. Not funny,
what do you mean, we respond, the
gold is there for us. The sand we
take we put back; no one can tell
we've been there. Not phallic, the
dredge is kitchen spoon, shovel, key
to a locked chest. A small engine,
40 feet of black four inch hose,
a good water pump, six feet of
sluice pan with 30 riffle bars.
We tighten the screws, straighten the
riffles, arrange a carpet along the
sluice bottom to miss nothing, push
gently into the sounding narrows.

147

4. Working the River

Finding just the right bar is art; we
park the muddy truck in old linden trees,
the river between granite cliff and a
placer steep downslope, thin ice on the
surface. We carry the dredge in pieces
over the gravel to the water, cold
echoes back and forth, gloves and hoods.
Long boots on, I enter the icy Similkameen,
bending, with the hose, to the clear
flowing water, disturbing what has not
been disturbed, tickling the sweet river,
urging an appearance. The small engine
violates the silence, water and sand
through the hose to the sluice pan,
the riffle bars, the rushing sound of
gold? Working the river, sweating,
black wiggling hose, clear cold, bent back,
more sand, more sand, whisshing whisshing
water, dredging the Similkameen.

5. The Abandoned Mine

Rests silently near the sounding river,
shaft and crusher building sloped upward,
wooden, paintless, tailings all to one side.
Zinc, magnesium, silver? We don't know.
Not gold, that's certain;
too glittering an array for gold.
No one around, just the river,
trees, cliffs, stray echoes.

We're quiet around such a mountain fact;
dreams like ours solidified her.
Leave her as she is,
two or three birds flitting in her eaves,
the hiss and rumble of water nearby.

148

Joseph Powell

Dreaming Parsley, Winter Soup

1

Dead people call to us in dreams,
they're lonely to come back
and wear the clothes of the living.
My husband thinks it's foolish,
says we're dumb as carrots,
heads down, dreaming parsley,
digging deeper every day.

On our first date he said
he was best at órt iculture,
I loved the way he said it,
though it was his father's
run-down farm he loved.

I should've suspected sooner.
Three months ago his army friend drowned—
for two seasons in France
they trusted only each other,
but he couldn't remember his face,
the color of his hair.

What of me?
My eyes, my breasts, my winter soups?

Some Sundays there was hope
which rose like doubt with his pipesmoke,
the cat snoring in his lap,
a silence that remembers me.

Now he comes in from the fields
weary from thinking alone
over the monotonous furrows,
scarcely able to see
the food steaming before him.

2

This afternoon I sat in a chair,
coffee turning to smoke,
the TV turning blue in its corner,

and watched the river
wave the thin arms of aspens
because they looked into it:
the branches burst into sticks,
fell together, composed,

burst again, arguing.

He says she's left for good,
yet I try to imagine the woman he'd seen:
dressed in furs,
she walked along this river,
stopped, glanced down
and stared into the water,

into branches breaking about her head.
She's the mystery that men love
who only loves herself.

She drifts into silence,
entirely alone
in the beauty only she can imagine.

3

When I woke last night,
my hands ached from being fists.
The sheets shone like moonlit snow,

my husband's face was painted
with an innocence I'd never seen:
his hand curled and fat on its pillow,
his breathing a child's.

I wanted to wake him,
to walk down to the river
and watch the moon drag
its white gown across the water.

I believe he loved me once.

Our lives aren't beautiful,
time sours in our mouths,
though in the fields he could believe
anything might grow,

then lies sprouted like winter wheat,
kept alive by snow,
his own parsley dreams.

One day I'll enter his dream
like that woman along the river,
robed in all I could not be,
stand in his eyes blooming
like a rose in the snow,
and he'll wake, dazzled by what he's seen,
to lie for hours afraid to touch
the cold in the sheets around him.

Leveling Grain

Imprisoned in a tin silo
I leveled grain with a scoopshovel.
The auger was a faucet
pouring from the one
shaft of daylight.
Shirtless, I shoveled
the wheat mountain
in the silo's dark
until all my hairends
were coated with blond dust.
I spit mudwads
and sweat made dirt streaks
on my chest.
I kept thinking of water:
the blue behind the dust-window
got closer than an ultimatum.
Finally, I rounded the hill
in the center and climbed out.
The clear coolness,
a dive into a lake of air.

I let the breeze pass over,
my nipples gooseflesh,
and reached for
the gunnysack waterbag.
Water leaked over
the corners of my mouth,
ran down my chest,
leaped the lip of my pants.
Standing there,
looking out over the fields,
the bag dripping,
I thought of all the years,
the centuries of people
breathing the grain's dust
under a hot sun—
Joseph & the Jews,
Gentiles and Indians,
Chinese and Africans,
the long human chain
that linked me to them;
and of all the coins or promises
spilling from their fingers
like grains of wheat.

I saw the past emerge,
enlarge like some ancient
seagod from a sea of grass.
It was immense,
its slick, endless tail
thinned into the horizon.
The air was soundless
and I was only
a part of the earth
beside a silver flash of light
seen from an airplane.

On Finding a Homestead

Angular, crosshatched in shadow,
its bleached boards sun-curl.
Now it's the wind that rearranges light.

Odors of summer sage and decay,
a Prince Albert can nailed in the outhouse,
suggest the family's walks up the close hill

to check the few cattle the land could hold,
or the distant Stewart massif
floating like a crowd of sails on the wrinkling air,

how they went on as usual:
more sage burned, rocks moved, water hauled,
as wide troughs of land rolled yellow.

Whatever pain or love they knew, or could have known,
whatever hand came out of the dark
and blessed or denied their seed, their bread,
it lit the fire every night,
kept watch over the rainbarrels set for the horses,
resolute & thoughtless.

Looking out over the fields,
they came to believe
the slow turning of the world

ground wheat into snow,
snow into wind, earth into flesh,
and nothing, not even rain, was assured.

Steven Reames

Ghosts

As we pulled into the rest stop
one of my students asked,
"Do you believe in ghosts?"

I pointed
at the line joining
and breaking
the varied grey rock
from the solid blue sky,
at the exposed
thirds of hexagons
wrenched
in a rusty "U,"
and at the incongruous white below—
too white,
like paint,
bright white in the sun
coming over our shoulders.

Later I spoke
of my river-drowned friend
now necessarily present
in that place.

I did not speak
of my grandfather,
he merely chancing to be present
in the season
and in the sunlight.

And I did not speak of you—
though necessary,
and in the land.

I did not tell them of you.

Too essential to mention,
too real to be safe,
you haunt the Columbia
where it pushes through the Cascades.

The highway twists past basalt cliffs,
themselves twisted iron columns
supporting dark masses—
one era,
one flow below the next.

Mountainsides show
ranks of rock-flow
set at angle
long after hardening
now tilting inevitably
miles long into the river—
the ridgeline hard against the sky.

I saw you
this time
in the fall light
the sun pulled low
the grass on the southern slopes tawny
the oaks flaring in the draws.

But it was the same
last spring
in the softer, higher light
and the vernal greens.

And it was the same
the last two winters
in the storms,
the dark familiars of the Gorge,
faces and forces
of sky rock water
no longer nameably distinct.

And today
when I came to where you stood,
no less haunting in the flesh,
it was the same:
my end began
again;
I saw, but

I did not tell them of you.

Three Women

I step off the bus and
onto the powdered concrete,
missing the expected squeak beneath my feet:
cold too dry for sound.

The moon is not quite down.
Beyond the flat white and the square brick,
beyond the basalt and the rock-colored pines,
behind the above alpenglow haze,
the white disk hangs low
in Northwest January blue.

The shadows all point at the moon.

I turn to look at the sun—
straight back,
in opposition,
too far away for warmth,
but bright on the edge of the world,
the city, and dark hills—
lighting the air,
the mist,
the impossible pink clouds,
and, I suppose,
my face—
light, at least, in my eyes—
light that pales the moon.

The moon hangs still,
constantly unsteady.

As I walk the straight concrete,
I remember the river—
in front, behind, and sweeping
all around—
fast, dark, cold, and far below.

Franz Schneider

Little Spokane River: Indian Paintings

Rocks rise from the hill
And wall the river forever.
The swirling eddies
Shake the guardian trees
That mark the sacred place.
There the center is still.
The sun runs faster in its track.

Cleaving resistant waves,
A man made land by the rocks.
He painted this red sign
When the deathbird called:
Here by the thundering water
I am safe in the circle of earth.
We are each other's work.

Mt. Stuart: North Ridge in October

Rockfalls drive me into myself.
Jack Lake below is a dream.
I lift my head and wait.
Only the runes on the North Ridge stare back.

The icy downdraft blows snow in my eyes.
I think of eagles and hawks.
All day I have not seen a bird.
Why did I come here?

Now I am stopped by glacier and wind.
The frost has swept the granite clean.
I close my eyes:
Upon what signal will the rock wall crumble?

Priest Lake in August

Jutting into the lake,
But tethered to the bottomed dark,
The old dock rises and falls,
Noiselessly rises and falls,
As it rubs its gentle flanks
Against pilings of cedar
And rides the steady up and down
Of currents blown landward
By the cool night breeze.

I hear the tree tops sway
On the hillside above.
From the distant shore,
A few lights probe the night
With slender finger tips.
Somewhere in her cabin,
A woman reads a book.
A man rigs his gear
For deep fishing in the lee
Of the Selkirk Crest at dawn.

We listen to Lyra playing
Late summer tunes overhead.
Neck extended and wings spread,
The Swan silently trumpets its song
Towards midnight where well-fed
And head high, Pegasus gallops
Through meadowed horizons,
His hooves striking sparks
From ridges of mountains until
The sky flames and rains on us
A shower of glittering stars.

Travelling East I-90 in the Fall

Tilting upward past Whiskey Dick
Mountain, brown fields sweep
The horizon, then tumble off the edge.
Great flocks of birds swing up and out,
Circle, and dip down for grain
The combines left along the ditch
That irrigates the land near Ellensburg.
My road points East as I accelerate.
The motor vibrates from the stress
Of fighting both the incline and the weight,
Though this time neither children
Nor their gear loads down my aging car.

I make the railroad bridge with ease
And pass beneath its steely web
Of girders balanced black across the void.
The curve swings me past dry land farms,
Shielded from flashfloods by a dike,
Where yearling herds without a memory
Bunch up in sagebrush covered draws
And stiffly wait for fall round-up to start.

I feel the presence of the fields out there,
Steeping rose-colored in the setting sun.
And then, a witness moment out of time:
The rearview mirror signals Mt. Ranier—
Its snowy flanks, a tinge of summit red—
Until I top the rise of Ryegrass Pass
Ten miles from Vantage where I hear
The hoarse cry of a Western crow.

Below and East, I see large open tracts
In thickening gloam. The farmers burn
The seed fields clean. They seem to float
From earth, those fields, and slowly rise
Into the sky where once I saw a winter moon
Shine on this vast and glinting land
Of wind-voiced distances adrift with snow.
That was at Christmas time, two dozen years ago.
I ferried family through here:
The night air was a watery sea, waves lapping
Fields for endless miles, until they reached
The farthest shore of Frenchman Hills.

Suddenly, skidding on the ice.
A crash: The sound as when tall timber hits
The ground, the treetops breaking off.
A crumpled hulk slides to a stop.
Scattered debris trails in its wake.
The foreign car, just passed before our eyes
With newly-weds so eager to arrive,
Was hearse before we reached the wreck.

The bridge at Vantage is at hand.
No time for requiems it says. God only
Knows the faces of the dead. I slow
My car. To cross the river here, you make
Concessions to the wind. From shore,
A covey of late quail explodes and veers
Across a downstream stubble field,
Then vanishes in all that brown.
No time to watch. The bridge in seconds
Issues in a curve that rising leads me
Up the hill to Moses Lake
and then past Ritzville home.

Molly See

Burned Out

I want to go
where the sun doesn't shine on glittering snow,
away from children and their sleds
and friends with their Christmas water beds

to the mirk and drip of Oregon.
I want to wake in the green wash
of cedars,
where rain runs down my window
and a frog sings under my room.

No reason to get up. I won't care
if the kids have cookies in their lunch,
or brush their teeth
or even brush their hair.
Maybe I'll cook oatmeal for my old mother.

I want to scrape red candle wax
from a dark oak table,
gather cobwebs on a broom;
while apple logs drip and steam on the fire,
read a book I've read ten times before.
I want to walk through the fumes of Greyhound busses,
and drink coffee at the counter with strangers:
the woman who carries a box of apples
to her niece in The Dalles.
The man from Wenatchee whose daughter
just got divorced for the third time
and lost her driver's license.

I want to lean on a bus window
and watch horses standing in snow
waiting for hay,
then standing in mud,
then lying on dead grass in the afternoon sun
somewhere south of Yakima.

Daylight Saving

We're driving north to Dartmouth,
my Grandfather's school, unwinding
Spring on a slow reel;
light green leaves are shrinking in the woods,
flowers disappear.

None of my family in the West have made this journey
to see where the bronze book-ends, the rug,
the picture of the team of 1910 came from.

We ride alone in a light rain.
I sleep and dream of a day
before we were married;
when I wake and see you driving
thirteen years have gone away as clean as cellophane.

We drive together through calendar farms.
Morgan horses lean on fences.
In a wet field
a man undoes the work of beavers.

It's late when we reach the old town.
You call Judy, who keeps the children—
"It's O.K.," she says,
"You know, time has gone up today."

Sleeping Over

Red speckled cookies, pale on a plate
made me think of her place,
some Christmas Eve in the back of my mind;
her house on the dark river-cliff,
a light from her kitchen.
Fathers were there, then.

In summer, lizards by the back door;
jars of cherries line the way down
to the room where her brother sleeps
like a troll by new diggings.

The night-train from the river
rattles her bedroom window; in the dark
the whole house shakes, but she sleeps.
I dream I'm falling off the rock wall
over cliffs and water.

The stone play-house where we mixed
mud and cobwebs in a broken pan.
The woods, full of blue-bells, rocks and poison oak.
The pond that swarmed in spring with little frogs
we stepped on.

But mostly about the house—
something made me afraid;
smells. Milk cooling in pails.
Old butter in the cupboard.
A dripping deer hanging somewhere.
Her lawyer-father up in the attic
loading his own shells.

Summer School

I The School

After morning prayers in the old church
we wind single file to the Oak Street School,
newly oiled and waxed. We drowse,
crickets simmer on the playground,
while sisters find connections
in the sacraments; we crayon yellow
red and purple stripes
on the robe of many colors.
Stumbling out of the dark
incense after Benediction
we wait for a ride home;
orange poppies
burn like votive candles in the sun.

II The Sisters

Once a year they came to dinner at our house;
black on green they swooped and ran in the smooth back yard
batting the shuttlecock back and forth.

Each afternoon we sang together,
feeling *Tantum Ergo Sacramentum*
like a spell that fell apart when they were gone.

On the last day they gave us treasures;
pictures of a gilded sky
where holy women in their long brown hair
and silver robes
stand on the stars.

The same four nuns came back each year.
We always wanted Sister Mary Michael Francis;
she played baseball
better than a boy.
She wanted us; I guess
that's why they sent her somewhere else
to learn humility.

When It All Comes Together

Once on a late afternoon in November
my children and I rode into an orchard.
The time allowed us was short
between school and dark.
We snatched yellow apples left over from harvest,
Water-cored, hard, tasting like wine,
sour and then sweet.

We rode three mares:
my daughter on a sorrel,
my son on Shammie,
and I on a big appaloosa.
We rode along slowly, bareback. They were ahead.
The round brown haunches of Shammie moved smoothly.
My daughter's red hair hung down, exactly
the red of her horse's mane.

All around us the trees were pale yellow,
as big and ghostly as the wings of a stage.
The grass we rode on was tan.
Why was it so soft? Lady was moving so strongly
and smoothly beneath me it seemed like a dream.
I looked at the grass.
It was dead, piled up inches deep.
It seemed like it had been cut for us to ride on that day.
In the time between complaints and judgments,
lessons in haltering and closing gates,
we rode in silence.

John P. Sisk

An Aviary

I

Wallace Stevens fancied the blackbird,
Which, unlike insurance policies,
Could be looked at thirteen ways.

II

Poe liked the raven, probably
Because however you looked at it
It wasn't very talkative.

III

Shakespeare liked the lark
But saw it only one way:
Singing at heaven's gate.

IV

Wordsworth was ecstatic about the cuckoo
Even though, being an insomniac,
He hated lying awake listening to it.

V

Tennyson admired the crooked clawed eagle,
Probably because it anticipated the dive bomber.

VI

Shelley was high on the skylark,
Unlike Byron for whom,
Even when he was high on gin,
No birds sang at all.

VII

Coleridge liked albatrosses, I suspect,
Because they made good pendants.

VIII

Eliot and Keats favored nightingales,
Always singing in someone's sacred wood
Or fading romantically into the forest dim,
Where they bothered no one
No matter how you looked at them.

IX

Hopkins admired the windhover
Because it was so Christological.

X

Whitman liked the thrush because,
Singing in the swamp,
It reminded him of Lincoln.
To him one bird in the swamp
Was worth thirteen birds in anybody's bush
Even if nobody was looking at it.

XI

Emily Dickinson adored robins, orioles,
Hummingbirds and even blackbirds, provided
They ate their angleworms raw,
Which involved a way of looking at them
That Stevens never thought of.

XII

And to Yeats birds meant so much
That he wanted to be one—a gold one, if possible:
He dreamed big.

XIII

Poetry, apparently,
Is for the birds.

Sea Prospect: Georgetown

This aerated and stilted place,
Where each roof and wall and shutter
Warps and rots like timber under water,
Is an ageing prostitute whose face,
Gone slack and haggard, is left grieving
(Enchantment's dreariest parody),
Her makeup spoiled with tears for beauty's leaving.

Here to the Atlantic the Demarara
Drags the jungle, and the sea's eaves
Are upland mud that the waves riffle,
Mold, and leave when the tide leaves.
Egrets, fire crabs, and gulls
Swarm over the beach, and native bathers'
Black heads bob. Smacks with dirty sails
Stand at the ocean's rim. And there high
Over the northwest an old dragon gathers:
And the smoke-gray skirts and trailed veils
Of the squall drag over the gray sea.

Sea Prospect: Palm Beach

The heave of her is time's muscle,
Tumid from a clenched hand
Too strong for fingerhold
In mere sand.

The deep green of her is greener
If a wave break
Or a gull's wing or a sail
Flash white for her green's sake.

Her sinewy but rare voice
Is thewed with the surds
Sea wall, rock, and sand
Shape her tongue to for words.

The gray pelican on the jetty,
Frozen in cogitation,
Poses a question mark
Over her immutation.

And her amorous apple-breasted
Vestals, oiled and biscuit-brown,
Lay their holy hours entranced
Till her votive sun goes down.

The Inadvertence of Being

As in October after
a day that is all gold
Suddenly the late sun
Loses its grip on the air
And the chill, winter-whispering,
Settles on mum and dahlia:
You wonder, did the summer
Leave because you'd forgotten
That only your close attention
Could keep it with you always?

As when a child you thought
That if in a dream you saw
Some wonderful thing, all gold,
And seeing it there remembered
To hold it desperately tight
You'd wake with it yours to keep:
But a child in a dream forgets
And wakes with empty hands.

Ruth Slonim

Countables and Unaccountables

(centennial musings)

Millennia are countable
by breaths drawn and expired,
by centuries of plus and minus,
        poignancies afire.
Vision prods the future
through a magnifying past
detailing lost and found,
fertilities and infertilities of ground,
undertows of swollen pride,
games of seek and hide.
On ego-trips some lose their way
quantifying night and day.
More modest venturers discover
eloquence in humble folk
who occasion sweet surprise
sharing sensibility,
widening dull eyes.
Ready warmth and inner spark
illuminate the enigmatic dark.

Easy come easy go insights,
blaring violence in televised fare
disorient innocent travelers
heading for music unheard.
Where, oh where, is that mythical bird?

Hope, thought to be blind, is eternally
        young,
nurturing dreamers and dreams.
Blind strategy with a heavier foot
concocts Machiavellian schemes.
Purveyors of "image" buy and sell
castles of sand in a golden clime,
exacting exorbitant price,
devaluing essence as nickel-and-dime.

      "All aboard for the next
          Shangri-La,
      the next ingenious wizard
      devising the next Hurrah!"

Gardens of knowledge make welcome
those who would eagerly grow
as the recurring spring flower
            emerging from snow.
Countering distrust and malignant terror
compassionate earthlings score war
            the ultimate error.

From their present-tense perch
viewers attend a play in one act.
What of the fluent continuum,
mystery flowing before and thereafter?
Where the empathic tears
and all-embracing laughter
to groom earth's disheveled family
            far-flung and diverse
for the next centennial chapter?

    Integrity mounts a stern steed.
Agile equestrians spring to this need.

Cosmic Grammar

Split Infinity:
        to be
rent asunder
by atomic thunder.

Desert Flowers

Nubs of cactus prickle into bloom.
Day blossoms too, red-orange and heavy.
    Heavy the decimated fruit
        hanging in memory
        and in prospect.
    Hotter than heat of desert
    this mushroom-burst of flower,
        this tainted hour.

Gerald E. Tiffany

Birthday Card to One's Self

—for G. T.

Take a short stock of what you have, O Self—
another twenty years if you still smoke,
a liver hotter with each soaking night,
a rusted truck, crumbling walkup,
and leaping Olivetti.
You are my own formed urn, well wrought,
or rotten through debauch,
word flinger, bird guesser, friend maker.
You are butterfly-eagle, patient spider cat, bat feather.
You are watcher-waiter, whiskey namer, tamer of paperbacks,
destroyer of dust motes, thumb wrestler,
ripping it up through another year, proposing toasts.

> (Walking home at night I see
> each nascent moment caught,
> shining like freshwater pearls—

In the Effigy, in the Serpent's Eye

—for Janelle

> "With tremulous cadence slow, and bring
> the eternal note of sadness in." — Arnold

We do not know the songs
those builders sang,
but stay and listen now,
you who came home with me
to this land's heart:
a land of storms
between the greatest rivers.
Listen hard, woman
of far conifer woods,
of granite and ocean.

171

Before Oglala Sioux
fought to the grassy sea
from the red South,
even before the Sak and Fox
heard of Missouri or Iowa,
old tribes fashioned with river silt
great effigies of animals
as homes for death
and tributes to all life.
They saw the power of symbols,
those first farmers,
first pedestrians.
But we know nothing
of them save for shards,
some cobs and ashes,
and these effigies,
mounds shaped like eagles and foxes,
covered with flowers.
Uncork the wine we carried on the path;
we'll pour a little on strange graves
and drink the major part.
Then I'll stay sitting here
in the serpent's eye of this effigy,
happy to be sad
on this grand floral tomb
until you see the way
pedestrian enough
to call me from shadows and dog tooth
violets, from marsh marigolds.

Where bear once traced
the Mississippi's throat,
now forests become woods.
But here grow wild roses still,
the trillium and columbine
by the willow stumps,
and deeper hide morning glories
and the white blood root.

My heart lies low with these flowers,
the line I've been waiting to say,
the reason I've teased you here
to ancient effigies,
to this rare stand of butternut,
of shag bark hickory,
great burr oak,
of elm, cottonwood, walnut.
The heart itself is deciduous,
and holds a hope fragile
as this sedimentary land.

Last night I dreamed of you,
and you became the rich,
lightning-charged earth.
Cumulous now, these clouds
spawn twisters that grind
like bison herds, like my dreams.
Love, with these words
I've brought you back
to my heart's home.
Walk soft and easy here
in thunder, rain, and wind,
in the land of a poem
you asked for long ago.

Water Passage

for Keith Aubrey

West of Rat Islands, Aleutian Archipelago,
winds in williwaws, wildest gales;
seas running, swelling, chopping, sucking up ships;
cold, colder than freezing air.
Beyond the Alaskan Peninsula,
beyond Dutch Harbor and Adak,
flying the crescent, following islands
toward Attu, toward Russia's Kamchatka.

I look east at two seas
demarked by geysers and boiling troughs.
The Bering: blue as sky, blue
as ice, blue as a beluga's eye.
Pacific: green, green as gorse,
as moss, green as tundra in July.
Two colors, faces, personalities,
two souls perhaps in these seas.

I like to think these neighbors,
the blood of great currents in their veins,
the rapid heartbeat of the changing moon
thumping the cold chambers of submarine hearts,
their nervous systems leaping pods
of dolphins, sperm whales, schools of sharks,
and the smallest plasma of plankton,

I like to think these neighbors lovers,
and the wild line of their meeting,
that grand, crashing line of foam and spray
as gentle fondle, nuzzle and caress.

Call it pathetic fallacy then—
but remember how last winter,
ice just out of the lake,
we clung to a capsized skiff for half an hour,
anchored to death by parkas and winter boots,
weak from freezing,
the keel cutting into our hands.

What of the winter rainbow trout
fat from grazing bottom snails,
our game for a Sunday morning—
would they have had our eyes?

We live in retrospect, but death is now.
At the time I felt cold, feared
drowning, wondered if the rescue boat
would come up fast enough.

A cold embrace she gave us, Keith,
a passage from Saturday to Monday,
the focusing event

There are ways of finding water,
  of changing blood to water.

Patrick Todd

Country Wedding

All nervous in country lace the bride
rode down the mountain with her father,
wagon reins springing easy in the early sun
Fifty mums banked the church walls white
Thick cream candles   The groom sat
mute for the stiff picture,
both hands closed big as hammers

Women owned this time around the holy cake
The old fathers, faces puffed red
from years of whiskey and the blazing wheat,
waited out weddings like a funeral
Even the sleepy minister hated
circles of screaming kids and spotted
a yellow toy he'd love to crush

Gone the bride in white lace
whose wedding moon lit up a long lazy string
of geese over McGuinnigan's Pond
Now the farmers' sons grow mean in town
a boy beat a hole in a boxcar
with a hundred-pound furnace iron
Gone twenty horses steaming in the barn

For the Memory of Albert Mueller

Christmas Eve   Twin spruce glow
four-hundred blue bulbs at the cemetery
entrance   Six foot stones stand
straight as oak stumps under the pine
and slabs of forgotten names
are buried under mounds of snow
In the wretched winter of 1951, Albert
Mueller opened the school nativity
play, "This here is the story of Jesus"
That April one of the nuns dressed the top
of a first grade desk with two dozen
carnations white as goose down
Albert's youngest brother, Hans,

had climbed on the hood of an old Packard,
dropped inside an open chest freezer
and closed the lid   Hair cut bald
on the sides of his head, hands already
grown the size of rolled beef,
Albert stood at the grave site in his
thick, wool, funeral suit, his whole
family frozen with dead-pan stares
of German refugees stranded on a London
dock   Next to his brother's casket,
he might as well have looked up at waves
of bombers over Dresden for all he
could do to hold back the grief and loss
If his brown suit once fit some lost
uncle or grandfather   Or traded
for three silver dollars and a sledge
hammer at Wood's Second Hand
If it slept twelve years inside a trunk
and came out smelling of mothballs
and the smoldering fur of a dead muskrat. . .
No one cared that Friday at 9:28 A.M.,
exactly 29 above, and wet sod soaking
the shoes of everyone who waited
in the cold   Albert Mueller might have
stunned the world with one brilliant word
to save mankind from doom had he been asked
He wasn't   His dad, who held the arm
of Albert's weary mother for once,
led her away with the priest, and every
man, woman and child that morning
It was all we could do to get back
to the cars, to the weight of our own
lives and turn over the engines

Handout at Jacoy's

In a dead shop entrance on Main,
blown newspapers, three
wine bottles and a cardboard box
I walk by looking for my car and spot a wino
urinating on the brick wall
His buddy steps out of the shadows,
bumming change   Black hair thick
as a badger's, teeth busted off, and a wry
grin that would snake money from a child's hand
"Cherokee," he says, "I'm a full-blood
and Viet Nam veteran"
He follows me to Jacoy's News

where we meet the sullen
face of the owner
Another chump caring for the poor,
I might as well let the rain blow in, or have
my dog squat over the fresh mopped floor
Inside the glass cases,
round tins of tobacco, cigars

in yellow and white boxes,
and bright packs
of cigarettes gleam a miniature
carnival of colors   So the tramp stops
everyone in the place for a second
Hands spread on the counter, coat bagged open
like a small brown tent. . .
He dreams in the world of his own
time, and savors
his privilege to choose

Michael Gripping Satan's Hair

All old schools have the same smell
Food from the big kitchen
and wood floors lit with fresh wax
When I was a kid the desks were bolted to flat skis
Chalk dust stained the blackboards with endless blizzards
and our first-grade teacher swatted our butts
with a two-foot hose   Mornings she
folded down map-size pictures of Adam and Eve
Christ wept in the suffering garden and Joseph stood tall
and beautiful in this bright colored coat
Thieves from the bushes attacked and left him
in the sand   God and evil

planted deep in our small hearts
I remember ball coat
book cup and words about Dick and Jane
Mostly they played on grandfather's little white farm
New car Brand new barn and the whole family
happy together with perfect hair

Our fathers drove old beaters
to the smelter Abandoned
mothers drew monthly welfare and Bonnie
Deshner got "knocked up" in eighth grade
One Indian kid lived alone with an old old man
No wonder the giant pictures filled with pain
In the best one St. Michael leans down raising his sword
for the big swath, Satan's
hair locked firm in his other hand

Waking in a Train Yard

Morning sun and the mint green maples
Frost on the grass and it's May 5th
Frost on the train engines and ice gleams
along eaves of the roundhouse
What's it like to wake cold in a boxcar?
To roll over   Slide down   To find frost
on the sway-bar and couplings
Last night another tramp walked the yard
till his feet swelled inside his boots
and he laid down in wet grass
wishing he could crawl inside the ground
Wearing a big army field coat, he sits down
in a cafe this morning and orders coffee
Imagine the first cup poured in a white building
before Christ, probably in Venezuela
Coffee beans the color of brown skin
They are the brown of Moroccan dowry beads
Trappist rosaries   Of genuine Mahogany barstools
The licorice black espresso beans are heaped
in bags on coffee wagons like a cache
of raw money   Still coffee is the one
thing that allows a break from the cold
for a dime and five nickels.

*

Hair, snarled radish leaves   Eyes,
dead to the world   Finally in a warm place
the man sits with both hands around walls
or a porcelain cup   Imagine asking
him questions concerning Poland or the pope
A month back the president was shot
Imagine asking the man about violence and divorce
Once in a window in San Francisco, he found
grapes heaped with apples and bananas
With big purple eggplant, oranges, pineapples
and avocados sprayed wet next to smoked salmon
Smoked beef   Roast duck   Huge cakes of cheddar
and provolone   Salami hung overhead
with long coiled tubes of Hungarian sausage
And nudging thick walls of a tank, six
lobsters waited to be split open like giant
pistachio nuts   Outside the delicatessen
rich smell of coffee filled the street

*

179

To a man who sleeps on the ground, in cars,
under warehouse docks and in all-night laundromat
chairs, chatter in cafes sounds like chickens
It sounds like someone rattling tinfoil,
or the jumbled rantings of displayed televisions
In his whole life the man in the cafe has never
uttered a word concerning the mayor or Queen Elizabeth
He lifts his cup and the steam alone is worth
the first dime paid   Coffee   Coffee without eggs
Without buttered toast   Or a slice of ham
shaped like North Dakota   There are endless
stories about soldiers marching to their death
Endless stories about their women who waited
This poem is about bandages unraveled, raw sores
dry now   Blue and yellow harbor pillars
rise in fog above the lost boat   This morning
the man bummed thirty-five cents hardly asking
And if he thought about it, this moment suspended
in time is worth more than three long nights in bed
with sheets   More than coat and boots
of sheepskin   For this moment off the street
with coffee, he'd pay the last gold
coin raised from the bottom of the sea

Georgia Toppe

Following the Clearwater

Where the cliff holds back the river
and pines thicken their age,
I am seven again, my arms open and eager,
chasing the last white angle of day
into the silk way October has
of climbing the moon.

Some say we play this game forever—
catching the sun, letting it go.

But I do not let go.
The light frees itself, leaving behind
my body—a strange Indian shadow
carved on stone.
The image moves, it speaks,
it gathers sacred symbols—snakes, shields,
ruby beads to hang around my neck.
I lift my hands to the gods and wait
for the sun again,
my fingers outstretched
and trembling with the knowledge
one more summer has escaped.

Rumors of the last rain
still haunt the slow coming of the cold.
What rain has done to willows
the wind crawls in long, thin whimpers.
At the edge of the wind
winter is plucking
the stolen nerve of something dark.

Now the moon shivers in the dark of trees,
and under the trees, the night,
and under the night, the Clearwater
moving the earth's shadow.
Now in the river
I cannot find my face,
only a voice learning an old language.

An uneasy sky
traces the spine of the mountains,
their muscles taut,
their black flanks heavy with matted fur.
I call home, or forget,
inhaling the ancient breath
of camp smoke, of Appaloosas branded
by earth, by snow.
Challenging the Bitterroots,
my blue-wet bones catch fire.

Three Poems for an Autumn Birthday

I.
The Gum Tree

Along the river branch
birds reveal their cover.
The old oak stirs with wing rushes
and ancient September sounds.
Here a blue fleabane,
a goldenrod limp with blooming.
There a morning glory
half-open to the sun.
Ironweeds come brown. On the ground
the bittergreen odor of walnut hulls
infiltrates the leaves. But mostly
it's the stain of slow thin air,
the brittle rumors in the cornstalks,
the impatient urging chill.

I've heard stars intrude on such a day
and the earth answer
with sparse dark fingers terribly upward
uncolored, unclosed.

A sea so huge of shadow
rolls over the field
I can touch it, drown
as one might drown
between the canvas and the brush,
or in the afterhush
of breath before applause.

A solitary reaper shuts down for the night.
A crow caws.
The gum tree shivers, suddenly red.
My eyes paint it there, then,
that sunset, that cloud.
Perhaps I've known too many autumns.
The brilliance is in the dying, now.

II.

Long Distance

We are so huge
touching like this.
We are singing, you and I
over the sea,
and if the sea knows or does not know,
we only softly care, like dreamers
waking to each other.

> *Tell me autumn*
> *isn't a time of death*
> *after all,* you say.
> *There is night in England...*

Here the sun sits on empty nests.

> *rain, and cold.*

Cinquefoils still lace the meadow,

> *I read "Fern Hill" and dream...*

the legends...
> *of green.*

I want to tell you
how my son and I
chase leaves along the river,
skip stones below the rapids, the water
laughing upward where they dance. . .
how we watch river spiders
glide into each other, race nowhere
and back again.
I want to tell you
the river keeps calling your name.
But there's so little time.
Instead, I say

You speak faster than I imagined.
We have no rain.

High up where the smells of dying
trail the blue dry wind,
wind barely understands,
barely remembers
we are young as blackbirds,
young as the voices of their shadows
dream October
all the moon long, dream
slowly where the trees come loose
of leaves.

III.
Fall's a Beginning
The mountains flamed
that cold burn of October.
Winter paths found space
through the tangle of green
gone dry. There was still time
for the stream to go secret,
the pond to ice over,
those gray days to thicken
with snow.
But the air understood.

Do the trees realize their nakedness,
feel the cold? I asked once.
That was the first silence of love.

As pre-morning fog lifted,
softened the sun's plunge into the valley,
we watched a hawk circle
and dive,
heard the strike
hardly louder than the stars going out.
Light bathed our bodies, our hair.
A white flame, a root, a dead moon.

We walked on through a clearing
limp and brittle with fall.
Still heavy, yellow chestnut boughs hung low
where earthheat rose to winter scents,
wrapped our touching like a gift.
I could see the cabin up ahead,
the smoke curling.

Behind the cabin, the old logging road
stooped, then climbed deep into high,
high where the trees stopped
and the earth bore the wind alone.
And that was the loudest silence
of love.

Mary Ann Waters

Fishing the Jocko

But it's Anna's birthday and we've come fishing
with lawnchairs, crackers, champagne,
and we'll go home with photographs—
Ruth, shooting the cork with her thumbs
into the *summer, summer* of the river,
Anna, with the largest imaginary fish
ever taken from these waters, a beauty
twice the length of her arm,
and Mary Ann, up to her neck in a pool
so cold it takes her body
with her breath, and everyone

singing happy birthday, here's to champagne
in the sun, to one more year
that got away, here's to the flash
of uncaught fish, to tender mouths,
to the gleaming, forgotten hook.

Glasses

for my mother

I would have run out into the road.
I could see them there,
the gold rims, the curved
earpieces, the lenses
reflecting the mercury vapor light,
the intervals of neon
from the Mill Tavern.
In that instant
the eyes of the future
peered through those glasses,
opaque, on fire,
and I saw the car
not able to slow, I was waving,
it was a violation
of everything intelligent, the sudden
swerving, the almost beautiful
spray of light as the tires
shattered the glass, spun
the frames across the gravel,
the *no* held in my throat,
no, there was nothing
I could do, you waiting
in the parking lot wondering
how they could have fallen
out of our car like that,
how anything so fragile
could survive such traffic,
it wasn't a *life* after all,
just a pair of glasses, bifocals
with their tiny lines, their way
of making the world
clearer and bigger.

Seeking the Elements

He would leave the family waiting in the car,
leave them to stretch, the motor to cool,
and he would stride into the forest
to cut a forked willow branch,
                       peel it,
until it smelled sweet and green,
felt slick in his hands,
had a life of its own.

187

Through the isinglass curtains
of the Star touring car
the children watched the willow
reach out like a probe,

                        their father's
black hair lifting in an unexpected wind,
and they shivered as the sun turned away
behind sudden fingers of cloud.

                        He paced
this way and that in concentric arcs
deeper into the trees, his shirt
whitened by shadow.

                        Who could know anything
beyond that forked, peeled stick
which led them all?
                        Then in the space

of a meadow, he would feel the first tug,
the voice of the water speaking
through the branch, and the branch
bending down.

                He would no longer be
anyone's father. For here was the place
where his heart met a planet's truth:
the exact place

where the willow wanted to become water,
the water to become sky,
the dowser to become earth,
the earth to become fire.

                (In memory of my grandfather,
                Paul Duesler)

Travelling Highway 97: Biggs Junction to Weed

for Richard Hugo

"This town, only a trucker could understand,"
I said last night driving into Biggs,
and I thought of you, trucker-laureate
of western towns—Dixon, Hot Springs, Perma,
Philipsburg—all of them seen best
through the lens of your poems.
We're heading west and south, leaving
Interstate 80 here for Highway 97,
the fast route to Mexico if you're from Spokane.
I've been this way before and know
you'd be at home in Shaniko, a few miles
down the road—a sign says Shaniko's for sale—
and Dorris, a sharp left turn of a town
with everything in collapse
but a neon toucan above an empty marquee.

Here in Biggs, the problem is not decay.
No grey wood monuments to anything.
Three motels, two restaurants, some houses
and service stations—crossroads of convenience.
The Columbia, blue-black, seriously swift,
rolls on below this place and no one cares.
What happened centuries ago with wind and rock
and Indians and settlers moving west
is not remembered. And nevermind they say
that radioactive steelhead glow
from Hanford's plutonium waste,
conscience would mean hope, and hope
is not available in Biggs. No
history, no dreams. What counts now is
asphalt, diesel, gasoline, and cash.

As we enter the restaurant I pretend
you're leaning up against the counter
by the till, your scowl not quite breaking
into grin. *Find something here to love,*
you'll say, *or something to forgive.*
The waitress who brings coffee before we ask
will bless us, chill us, with a grace
that comes from years of loss.
Four good roads and a thousand ways
lead out of Biggs, remember that.

Or, *The birthplace of generic*, you'll say,
your voice so deep the word 'generic'
achieves the status of a god. *The God of*
Bland, the god who steps in, passionless,
when discriminations fail.
Just read the names, you'll add, the twinkle
in your eyes almost malevolent. *Dinty Motel,*
Jack's Restaurant, The Nu Vu Motor Inn.

We take it from there, invent a game proclaiming
Biggs the Greatest All-American Generic Town,
home of the mashed potato, canned tomato soup,
toasted sandwiches of Velveeta cheese.
The town bird, the sparrow. The color,
asphalt-grey so grey it's black.
The mascot, any mongrel passing through.
The motto: no shoes, no shirt, no service.
The obvious regret, no shopping mall.
It's always Tuesday, 5 p.m. in Biggs.
It never snows. No one plants a lawn.
No crime. Prairie dogs come here to die.

It's late. We choose the Nu Vu for the night
because we like the desperate yellow paint.
The rooms are cheap, the manager's direct.
"Sorry," he says, "tv won't be much,
reception's bad here all the time, mountains,
I guess, or power lines." We'd hoped for reruns
of B-rate films, a sitcom we used to dread,
but there are compensations: the drains
work sluggishly, the pillows are like shelves,
the single window opens to the parking lot below.
All night we hear the sound of trucks,
rapping down the grade. Three trains.
It's dark at 7 a.m. Cold winds from the gorge
rattle the exit sign.
                    Dick Hugo, heaven
had better be like summer in Montana.
I see you now in some forsaken, wind-blown town,
July, the weather blue sky and clouds in retreat,
the ripe fields shimmering in light,
the one or two remaining angels
overworked but willing to go on,
and some soul just arrived to say how much
you're missed. Not a get-together these days
without a Hugo story to pull us through.

Always, we hear the way your words held
praise and longing, all at once.
And we remember your generosity.
How you taught us to make each place our own
and then to love what was ours.

As you'd expect, Biggs Junction makes its claim.
Days later, in San Ysidro, just before the border,
in the pocket of my coat I find a motel key,
the Nu Vu Motor Inn, room 24. On the back
of the yellow plastic tag the directions say
"To return, drop this in any mailbox,"
                                         and I do.

Ronald Webster

At Saint Paul's Jesuit Mission

Stopping at the Kettle Falls pharmacy I
look for a birthday card I'll send Grandma
Webster coasting into ninety-three in a few days
finding one saying: you'll never be
younger than you are today, with a young
lady doing a furious jitterbug on the
card's red carpet rolled out for
this grandmother who dances
by her mere living; I
buy a 39 spiral pad, drive three
miles north to where I stand, leaning
on the Malibu, using for a desk the
car's black hard top, looking
through pines out to the Columbia
River below, a dark cold blue
sprinkled with asterisks' silver.
Overhead the sun is a silver
disc suspended at a pine's height,
the pine under which I walked ten
minutes ago, picking up a

pine cone the size of an
Ohio Buckeye; this Indian mission

founded by Jesuit blackrobes
in 1845
is a silent landmark of search
rising up as if Saint Ignatius
and Saint Paul were the only two
visitors in sight; I'm alone,
alone with these two visitors
unseen; Saint Paul's mission
church stands twenty yards
away, inside this aloneness.
An empty church.
An empty church whose stillness
is aloneness spreading out into
pine trees toward the river
disappearing in cold blue
waters. Aloneness
disappears in cold blue
this spring day of faint

chartreuse and a flood of feelings
undefined, flowing into pine
trees disappearing
in silence, cold blue like
blue ice islands floating in the
river; I'm alone,
standing on the earth
of a past Jesuit silence,
a past paradise cleansed by the sudden
strength of Christ's presence
surprising me in a lightning
quick satori
as if Christ is standing
by a tombstone rolled
away from the mission church
door, a tombstone rolled
over the bank's high
edge down into waters
of the Columbia, disappearing
in cold dark blue,
sinking into a school of waves.

Mount Spokane

Of some question's prologue I sing you
High among turquoise clouds, scarlet clouds,
Gold clouds threaded with these inks black
You read on the white of your seeing

Who, where, when, why I climb paths
Far into unknown beginnings,
Steps set on stone, steps set on the
Otherness of writing poems,

Steps set on crisp cataracts of sounds
You do not hear sleeping deeply
Among syllables marked coin
And curiosity, if you seek on Mount Spokane

The pocket coin minted whole
Universes full of stillness, galaxies
Given their Socrates, their Plato,
Their sprint into waiting a poem's

Millennia until these rhythms flow a
Grace you taste, pleased you
Know who's where when you've climbed
The white mountain, not asking why.

William Stafford's Question

journal: monday i got into the
malibu early in the morning
hungry for a breakfast
of first driving

to spokane,
carrying with me william stafford's stories
that could be

true and wanting them to be
at least plausible travel
companions which

they were
because
they are the geophysical origins
of man's soul

going toward the sound
creating your question; sixty
five miles down highway
395 i've got a hungry

curiosity for stack
of blueberry hot-
cakes at the ihop; i stop
forty minutes, read the

spokesman-review, look
through ads on the movies
in town; cannery row
and a bergman film; leaving, i

think william stafford's
steady poem on the earth
is enough soul for a walk
on spokane's skidrow.

Mildred Weston

Aunt Margaret

Past middle age she chose a pattern.
Burning leaves one year in autumn
she saw the width of summer tidily compressed
and took a narrowing habit as the best.

At war with all accretion, she never stored
on storage shelf: nor let a surplus fragment
lie about cluttering space, inviting dust.
She cleaned the cupboards out.

Matching the tight contraction of her house
she and her rooms became synonymous.
The features of her face grew angular
Thin thrift drew back the greying, scanty hair
and left her frame without a pound to spare.

Consumed or spent, she had so little with her
when she went. The neatest minimum,
the barest fraction.

I thought, although she failed
to beat subtraction at its paring game,
how close she came.

Biography

From my picture, taken when I was a child,
I try to trace from then to now
the journey of that young face
only half-knowing what took place
to make the difference a mirror shows.

Perhaps my father moved me,
or brother, friend or mother
in such a way that left a mark
still part of me today.

Roots put down in childhood,
vine or vein, whatever grasped the earth
established kinship with myself.
Living in darkness, these may be
the nightly comfort of my bed,
pressure of what someone said or what I read;
organic growth in growing old,
motion in brain and bone
turning from clay to stone,
changes of blood and nerve as they deserved.

Animal, vegetable, mineral—
of soul and body mixed—
time set the pins that hold me
here transfixed within my region,
finding what grace I can
standing at this place.

Birthplace

The dry lands hold me.
The stretch of long horizons—ample frame—
gives weight and structure,
tissue to my name.

Where Indian brush, years past,
painted basaltic cliff I move with rivers
curving through rocky outcrop
and tufts of scattered bunchgrass—
scant food for ranging horses—
through sage kept fast
by deep perennial root.

I wait with grain planted at hazard
in autumn, in arable furrows,
where grim wheat growers
gamble for rain on thousand-acre stands.

Full-circled plains
barren in winter, spare at best
place me in bitter grandeur
to live as the earth turns:
frozen in darkness, parched in sun
with horse rider and soil tiller
who bend to their obdurate master
the veering wind.

Dust Storm

Enclosure serves me well.
Pressure prescribes my girth.
Wrapped round by windy walls
I breathe a dusty breath.

Snatches of foolish tunes,
Ravelling bits of waste
Litter the island room
Whose air is motionless.

Apart from rage and rush
In storm untouched, untossed
By motion meant to move
Or vision to set to love

I stay behind the wind
And stinging thrust of sand.
My fingers strictly curled
Hold chaos by the hand.

Landscape

Scab land, they call it,
ridges of fissile rock and crumbling shale,
incrustation over earth-skin break.
No plow moves on where stone
proclaims stay clear.

Seen from the air the cultivated acres
barley, rye and wheat
stretch long and wide.
Fed by rain and river, field after field
brings grain, life-giver.
But dotted here and there
to ease the flow of growth
the scabs appear.

Beautiful fracture. See
thick rind turned inside out,
a hard revealing fact
the chronic wound and want
stubbornly not healing.

John Neal Williams

Border Crossing

"In '69 I was 21" (Jackson Browne)

love	as the vanguard we were pretentious	Berkeley
dope	unbound, experimental, sensational	Haight/Ashbury
groovy	and open to change	Monterey
peace	levitating freedom above success	Golden Gate Park
high	we ran naked together	Woodstock
psychedelic	into the nation's unconscious	Sunset Strip
hip	shaking its comfortable morality	Altamont

Sparks

I smoked yesterday's last cigarette
with the rising of today's sun

> twentyfour hours of road tar
> from the screaming red neon
> of Hennepin Avenue
> to the eclipsing solar hues
> of Immigrant Pass

and passed out sprawling across
the front seat of a broken dream

> the distance of an unending sky
> stretched beyond what should be
> seen as horizon to days passed
> and nights to come—while shadows
> distilled gauges and tattooed arms

from a day of flying over
plains, prairies and desert

> with nothing to pay attention to
> save arguments of jukebox pit stops
> and the solitude of pissing on sagebrush
> all along Interstate 80 I marked territory
> and paid bottle deposits unreturned

I bury a past I can't lose fast enough
on this exodus from midwest mourning haze

Fay Wright

Like Salt, We are Holy

We are the lovers who thrive
holding sky up and earth
all around, a quilt of praise,
yellow and blue,
the makings of green.

I am the woman who sits by the river
trailing one white hand,
a tarot ace,
all fertility and the gift
of waiting.

You are the man who leaps into air
throwing blue arrows,
shafts of light,
like the eight of wands
straight flying.

How we accommodate,
walk with legs parted,
and demand this force sustain us
like the field of mustard
in its positive yellow.

We are one church
on one hill, with one steeple
as we salt our eggs
and imagine the structure of yolk,
one red cell, multiplying
like a horizon of suns,
a year of days.

And dominion, our dew of heaven,
is the name we give,
the order we feed on.
And the birds rising now
and the water singing praise
and the stars lifted by our eyes.

From out of this song
we raise the wind like a house
that all have lived in,
that none have lived in.

Our dominion.

The Reading

Hugo, you bear,
cave-mouthed, you growled your poems,
and I was caught,
trapped by the stout paw
and sudden grasp.

What is it about the word,
smacked out the mouth
of the likes of you?
What is it about the poem?

A gambler with a palm of dice,
rattling against luck
against the odds until
"craps"
again—
a neurosurgeon with that knife,
slicing, oh so gently, the nerve
until the brain is complete—
it's not unlike poet
with the frantic pen,
scrapping against the page,
against the time
of not remembering.

I must not forget any sound.
But the odds are stark, are small,
and I know,
that driving back to work from the reading,
I saw what catches the pen,
stops the word.

I saw Lake Coeur d'Alene
beached in fog, shawled and enigmatic
in her silence, pine trees
dropping needles without sanction,
and an old man in mackinaw
pushing logs from the shore.
Silently involved in the task
of clearing summer beach of sign,
he strained the logs, end for end,
away, returning to the Lake
what she will not accept, yet
what will be lapped and swallowed.

He's never heard of you, Hugo,
nor does he care, as snow filters
onto the nearby hills and he
shoves out for winter.
But I move in
and out, like slippery logs,
from him to you,
and on the early road to work
I know the poem drifts
back to the shore
as surely as those logs.

The Shape of the Day

This is the shape of the day:
light, round; quilts, square;
the pine door, open wide
yawning on hinges
to the field of mares
whickering side by side.

We unfold like familiar linen
creased in old lines
and greet the day
happy to have chosen,
like the straight, white pines,
to stand upright and say

"Good morning, good morning.
Make the coffee black
the biscuits berry-blue.
Fill the white china cups with day
and the pack with room for a view."

This is the beginning of our time on earth
in love as graceless as the grass we trod
to reach the far barn, the birth of the red calf,
that bald face that blats the very air awake.

We are. *We are* in our black, rubber boots
that flap and take us to the last distant hill
where the morning star crowns our hope.

Come spring, come yellow and oat-green,
we hold to the top
to the light-cracked shape
of the day.

Robert Wrigley

Appalonea

Appalonea Miller Voisin (1840-1901)

There may have been a time when
your name went unnoticed: Amethyst,
Hortensia, and Emerald Maisie Hopes
were your chums, your names
sparkling off the page like so much paste
and silver plate. The Chinese
say you are not truly dead
until the last soul who knew your name
forgets it. Somehow we misplaced yours
against remarkable odds: a name
like a bird that sings its own,

or conjures up music
and hard fruit. Winesap, Golden
Delicious, the loud applause of wind
in the dry leaves of autumn.
But not a single shining image
of the human face. Grandfather's
grandmother, anyone we both knew
is dead now, and rooting
through certificates and microfilm
we've found every vital statistic but your face.

So I talk, and your name
is the only answer. Appalonea. Apotheosis
of appellations, a plum of pure sound.
Apollo, Apollonius, Apollinaire.
The great Johnny Appleseed
who gave us a peachy cider, a press,
and a pint of apple jack. I'm drunk
in the swirl of your name, the way
it applies to everything I see:
that strong grayish horse
across the field: Appaloosa,
a portrait but not a picture,
a prize, a poem, Appalonea.

Camping

I see my father camping, twenty-seven years
ago grappling inside the canvas bullet of a tent
he made with Harvey Winkleman, in their spare time,
working lunches and breaks, sewing a shell
around a skeleton of coded tubing,
between parachutes and the fancified guts
of the personal planes of generals,
every day through winter and spring assembling
a camouflaged and round-shouldered pyramid
in which they would sleep with their families,
their children and wives, for two
fleeting weeks of summer vacation in Yellowstone
or the Ozarks, or alongside some newly-made lake,
behind a dam, a smooth and miraculous monolith
made also by men, men like them
who could imagine one flood controlling all others,
who could see themselves as well in the summers
upcoming, camping: the laughter of children
hiding in the woods or swimming in the shallows,
wives lying on the docks in the sun
or stirring some stew, squatting in the blue smoke
from the campfire.

                       I see my father camping,
calling over twenty-seven years for one
then another of those numerically-coded poles,
all twenty-eight of them, his voice rising
toward madness, the clink again and again
of the flashlight falling from his shaking hands,
the wild shaking of the canvas walls,
shaking of the pine boughs by the wind,
and my shivering mother and sister, still
in the car and huddled up front around the heater.
I see us speaking little over dinner,
cooked and eaten in the meagre light
of the ancient Coleman lantern, the dinner instantly cold,
my mother shocked again by my father's temper
my father raging toward fun, believing
like so many of his countrymen in that time
of blind prosperity, in the things
he could fashion with his hands and mind,
in the wisdom of what came down to him
from the ones he'd elected, from the ones
who'd won the war.

I see my father camping
today, still devoted in his way to manufacture
and technology. Carefully he backs his trailer into place,
carefully he cranks his jacks, eases
the bubble of his level toward center.
He is old, he says, and deserves these
comforts, but I do not believe him.
He has always deserved his life, like the rest of us,
and now he walks with my mother along the trails
in the woods, across the beaches, and they look
like lovers. We're warred out,
he says, and he means his country,
and his rages he confines to a muttered obscenity,
a shrug of disgust for what passes these days for wisdom.
Retired, he thinks of his occupation as camper,
listener, and he understands at last what brought him
out of town. We look at one another through the smoke
of the campfire. We do not speak.
It is the quiet he strains to hear,
the noisy silence of another world he has grown nearer to
this late in his life. Damn the trailer,
say his eyes, it is just my tool!
Listen, another day is almost gone.

His Father's Whistle

For hours the boy fought sleep,
strained through the whirr of cicadas, moths
at the screens bumbling, night's
silver breezes, to hear out on the country road
his father's car rumbling in gravel.
He watched for the sweep of headlights
on the ceiling, a quick rush down
the driveway, then footsteps barely
audible over the lawn, his father's whistle.
Half a verse, a sliver of chorus, and his father was in
the house, quiet, the boy already drifting
in the night, asleep before the hand caressed his face.

It seemed to the boy that his life would be this way
forever, that out of the murmuring shadows,
the terror of distance, the danger of all
he did not know, there would come an order
like the one a melody imposed upon silence,
his father's among night sounds,
as though breath, a song,
and a boy's simple fear of the dark,
were a man's only reasons for whistling.

The Skull of a Snowshoe Hare

I found it in the woods, moss-mottled,
hung at the jaws by a filament
of leathery flesh. We have painted it
with Chlorox, bleached it
in that chemical sun, boiled loose
the last tatters of tissue,
and made of it an heirloom,
a trophy, a thing that lasts, death's
little emissary to an eight-year-old boy.

What should it mean to us now
in its moon-white vigil on the desk?
Light from the hallway makes it loom
puffball brilliant, and I look.
For no good reason but longing
I am here in your room,
straightening the covers, moving a toy,
and lightly stroking your head,
those actions I have learned to live by.

If we relish the artifacts of death,
it's for a sign that life goes on
without us. On the mountain snows
we've seen the hare's limited hieroglyphics,
his signature again and again
where we've skied. And surely
he has paused at our long tracks there,
huddled still as moonlight, and tested
for our scents long vanished in that air.

We live and die in what we have left.
For all the moon glow of that bone
no bigger than your fist, there is more
light in the way I touch you
when you're sleeping: the little electric sparks
your woolen blankets make together,
the shape of your head clear
to my hand in the half-light,
and this page, white as my bones, and alive.

Afterward: To My Fellow Readers

Now that we've read these poems, most of them at any rate let's say, we can reflect on where we've been and what we've seen. We have been on the road for a good while, moving from Floyce Alexander's poem that reflected on Mexico and offered to save our country to Robert Wrigley's meditation on fatherhood and death in "The Skull of a Snowshoe Hare." But reading a book of poems, perhaps an anthology in particular, is an odd sort of experience. We don't really ask ourselves what we've learned, hoping to answer, now I know how earthquakes happen, now I see why the South lost at Vicksburg, now I know how to adjust my carburetor. We don't even read poems to answer such supposedly "poetical" questions as: What is the nature of love? What is the meaning of life? Why are we mortal?

Why do we read poems? And, more specifically, why did we read this particular collection, an assemblage of poems that in some ways pertains to a certain limited geographical area? In reading these poems, were we surprised, or were our expectations confirmed?

In the August 1988 issue of *Commentary* critic Joseph Epstein confronts the first question in an article entitled "Who Killed Poetry?" Although he submits that "more poetry is currently being published than ever before" (15), Epstein argues that "contemporary poetry in the United States flourishes in a vacuum" (14). Poetry is rarely read, Epstein contends, "outside a very small circle," a circle that is increasingly "academic" at that, nourished as it is by creative writing programs and public poetry readings. Above all, Epstein laments the "professionalization" of poetry, which has resulted in poets writing primarily for other poets and in a loss of "spontaneity" that saps the power of language, leaving behind poems "chilled in the classroom" (20).

These are pretty hard words, and I certainly wish I could dismiss them out of hand, but I fear that much of what Epstein says is valid. If you've just finished reading through this anthology, chances are you're either a poet or a student or teacher of poetry. Poets do write for each other. To some extent they always have. But gone are the days when Byron's narrative poem, *The Corsair* (1814), sold 10,000 copies the first day and 25,000 the first month. Obviously his readers were not limited to poets and English profs.

You probably read this collection of poems because your own poems were included, because you knew one or more of the poets published herein, or because you were attracted by the local appeal of the anthology; that is, you expected to read about familiar places and about characters you could recognize as in some way representative of the area and about ideas and issues that concern you. If that is the case, you should not have been disappointed.

Epstein somewhat denigrates the lyric, which predominates in contemporary poetry and in this anthology, describing it as "a shortish poem ... generally describing an incident or event or phenomenon of nature or work of art or relationship or emotion, in more or less distinguished language, the description often though not always, yielding a slightly oblique insight" (19). Although "distinguished language" may be a misnomer for what attracts us to poems, it is surely "the way" something is said that appeals to readers of poetry. We cannot help being connoisseurs of language, even in an age when the language appears to be disintegrating, or perhaps especially in such an age. And that subtle, "oblique insight" is precisely what draws us to poems. There may be more, the appeal of what Robert Frost calls a "momentary stay against oblivion," but I think that is enough. Moreover, I believe this collection will have satisfied such an appetite.

Much of what we have read must have confirmed our anticipations regarding locale. Anita Endrezze writes of fossils at Vantage, Washington:

> what language is my passing
> shadow? my name is lost
> off the Columbia's cliffs:
> immersed in silica and water
> it will become an opal
> with a woman's soul

In "Idaho Vaudeville" Tina Foriyes writes of wheatfields,

> where the woman-shaped hills
>
> repeat
>
> "Wheat
> is but a grain
> in the harvest of this place."

Biggs, Oregon "makes its claim" in a poem by Mary Ann Waters, and in William Stafford's poems, Ronald Webster finds "enough soul for a walk/ on spokane's skidrow."

But amid the wheatfields, deserts, river gorges, and mountains we also encounter some surprises, for the poems are not bounded by their geography any more than the poets are limited in their imagination. Keith Aubrey's "Whalesong" obviously has no setting in the Inland Northwest, and Alex Kuo's "A Chinaman's Chance" looks back to Shanghai at the end of the Second World War. Madeline DeFrees's villanelle, "Keeping Up with the Signs," could be located wherever the meadowlark ranges. Most of us, after all, read for variety as much as for the pleasures of recognition.

That variety applies to matters other than place or subject. From the pencil thin lines of Randall Brock to the gap lines of Wes Hanson to the full margins of James MacAuley's "Letter to Richard Hugo from Drumcliff," the poets test the limits of form. And of course the voices vary. Note how quiet William Johnson is at the beginning of "Palouse":

> There is always an empty house
> by the road at the edge of town,
> its windows whiskered with lilac
> and letting in rain. . . .

The plain, simple ordinariness of the first couple lines sets us up for the impact of "whiskered" in the third. The conclusion of Linda Kittell's "Old Home Day" might remind us of William Stafford's observation that "A poem is a serious joke":

> . . . And every time
> Rhonda LaBombard serves dessert,
> we hold our breaths, wait
> for the button on that white cotton blouse
> to burst open
> and cool the air.

Editors of poetry anthologies are readers just like anyone else, though perhaps given to sometimes masochistic fanaticism. I have a good number of "favorites" among the over 200 poems in this anthology, but there are poems here that I really dislike. Moreover, a lot of the poems I could either take or leave. If someone asked, I would try to be evasive, claiming that certain poems just didn't "appeal" to me, or that others seemed "okay" but just didn't "intrigue" me. That is as it should be, I think. Epstein argues that creative writing programs are producing "more people who think of themselves as poets than this or any other country needs" (17). I suspect that no country "needs" poets, or if it does, maybe one is sufficient, or at most just one at a time. Let it be Homer, then Virgil, and so on.

But my suspicions aside, what I would *prefer* is that everyone be a poet. Why not? Suppose everyone were to start writing poems, and maybe even seeing them get into circulation one way or another. What is the worst that could happen as a result? In Sparta it is said that virtually all able males were soldiers. Did that produce a culture worthy of emulation? Is the quality of life better in those nations where all people are told to think of themselves primarily as "laborers"? What if we were all to become athletes? I suppose the worst that could happen if we were all to become poets is that we might bore each other to death. I think there are worse ways of dying.

Ron McFarland
University of Idaho
1990

209

BIOGRAPHIES

Floyce Alexander, author of two books of poetry, was born in Fort Smith, Arkansas and grew up in Granger, Washington, where his parents homesteaded at the end of WW II. He studied with Theodore Roethke and worked as editor-writer for Washington State University Press from 1963 to 1970. After two master's degrees (WSU, UMass) and a decade of university teaching, he has recently completed a Ph.D. in American Studies at the University of New Mexico.

Sherman Alexie is a Spokane/Coeur d'Alene Indian from Wellpinit, Washington, who is studying writing at Washington State University with Alex Kuo. His poems have appeared in *Cicada, The Eagle, Journal of Ethnic Studies*, and other publications such as *Windrow, Arete* and *Impetus*.

Chris Anderson, whose poems have appeared in publications such as *Crab Creek Review, Poetry Seattle* and *Greensboro Review*, was raised and educated (North Central High School, Gonzaga University) in Spokane, Washington. He is Composition Coordinator at Oregon State University and the author of *Style as Argument: Contemporary American Nonfiction*. Other publications include *In-Depth: Essayists for Our Time* (co-author); *Literary Nonfiction: Theory, Criticism, and Pedagogy* (editor); and *Tyranny of Virtues* (editor).

Keith Aubrey is a writer and college instructor in Spokane, Washington. His credits include publications of essays and poems in *Willow Springs, The Hollins Critic, Pembroke Magazine, Dog River Review* and *The University of Portland Review*. He is a founding member of Men Against Rape, Spokane, and a member of Amnesty International's Freedom Writers Network.

Dick Bakken was born in Montana, grew up in the Spokane Valley, and was educated at Washington State University. He authored several books of poetry and audio casettes, and his poems have been published in over 100 periodicals and several anthologies. He regularly toured the Northwest and the country as a producer and promoter of poetry, organizing poetry festivals and serving as poet-in-residence for colleges, state arts commissions, public school systems and prisons. Currently living in Bisbee, Arizona, he teaches at Cochise College and directs Heart of Carlos Spoken Arts.

Jim Bodeen teaches English at Davis High School in Yakima. He is the publisher and printer of Blue Begonia Press which he started after picking up an old C&P when the local paper switched to computers. Now he prints beautiful books on dampened Frankfurt, a mouldmade sheet from Germany, with covers of Mexican Bark made in the traditional way by the Otomi Indians. His chapbooks are: *Our Mother Blooming, Hammer & Praise,* and *Lockup.*

Jim Bradford was born in Denver, Colorado and moved to Cusick, Washington in 1972. Off and on, he has been publisher and editor of little magazines such as "Copula," "Copula Press," and "Copula Newsletter." He now lives in Spokane, Washington, where he works as a mailman.

Randall Brock lives in Spokane, Washington. His training was at Washington State University where he studied with Howard McCord, and at the University of Oregon with Ralph Salisbury. He has been writing and publishing for over twenty-three years, with eleven chapbooks and close to 350 publications to his credit.

Irv Broughton is a writer and filmmaker living in Spokane, Washington. His poems have appeared in *The Roanoke Review, Hollins Critic, Intro II,* and in his book, *The Blessing of the Fleet,* published by Lost Roads Press. He holds an M.A. in English from Hollins College, where he received an Academy of American Poets Prize, and is currently teaching Television Production at Spokane Falls Community College.

Bernadette Carlson has been engaged in college administration (President of Fort Wright College) and teaching (Professor of English) in Spokane, Washington for many years. Her poems, *Changing the Landscape,* appeared in 1983 and she is presently preparing a second collection for publication. She is a member of the Washington Province of the Sisters of the Holy Names.

Kent Chadwick is new to the Northwest. Having served recently as a Jesuit Volunteer at a community junior high school, Project Link, in the central ward of Newark, New Jersey, he now lives in Pullman, Washington, while his wife, Cathy, attends graduate school at WSU. He has completed two poetry manuscripts: *Still* and *Snow on a Crow's Beach.*

Sharon Clark-Burland is an artist and writer, living in Spokane, Washington. Her manuscripts, *Equivalent Meanings* and *O'Gushnahan,* are being submitted to publishers. She spent her early years on the Sault Sainte Marie Indian Reservation and several military bases. She was educated at universities in Japan, Massachusetts, Michigan and Washington State and worked as a reporter and newspaper columnist.

Gillian Conoley teaches in Eastern Washington University's M.F.A. program, where she is also the editor of *Willow Springs.* Her collections of poetry include *Some Gangster Pain* and *Woman Speaking Inside Film Noir.* Her poems have appeared widely in magazines across the country, including *The American Poetry Review,* and the *North American Review.* In 1988 she was awarded an Artist's Fellowship from the Washington State Arts Commission. She lives in Spokane, Washington.

Gary Cooper was born in Yakima, Washington and educated at Gonzaga University in Spokane. He received his Doctor of Arts in English from Idaho State University and taught eighteen years at Black Hills State College, Spearfish, South Dakota, specializing in creative writing, modern poetry and literary criticism. Some of his work during those years appeared in *Horizons: The South Dakota Writers' Anthology.* A permanent deacon of the Roman Catholic Church, he is now a pastoral associate at St. Augustine's parish in Spokane.

Tom Davis lives in Spokane and studies creative writing at Eastern Washington University. He has taught at Mt. Vernon High School, Big Bend Community College in Moses Lake, aboard PACE and in the educational opportunity programs of Western and Central Washington Universities. His work has appeared in *Jeopardy, First Person, Wire Harp,* and *Puget Sound Daily Mail.* He is also the organizer of the "Big Dipper" poetry readings in Spokane.

Madeline DeFrees, a native of Oregon, taught for many years at Holy Names College (Fort Wright College) in Spokane, Washington, where she published three books of prose and poetry under the name of Sister Mary Gilbert. Subsequently, she has held teaching posts at the University of Montana, the University of Washington, Seattle University, the University of Victoria, B. C., and the University of Massachusetts, where she was director of the M.F.A. program in creative writing. She is the recipient of a Guggenheim Fellowship and a writing grant from the National Endowment for the Arts. Her latest publications in poetry are *When Sky Lets Go, Magpie from the Gallows,* and *The Light Station on Tillamook Rock.* She has also contributed fiction to many reviews, as well as to *Best American Short Stories.* She now lives in Seattle, Washington.

Anita Endrezze has published poems, short stories, and art in many anthologies and magazines such as *Harper and Row's Anthology of 20th Century Native American Poets, Yellow Silk, Shaman's Drum, Willow Springs* and *Poetry Northwest.* Her work appears in West Germany, Denmark, Italy, France, Canada, New Zealand, and the U. S. She is half-Yaqui Indian and half-European and lives in Spokane, Washington.

Tina Foriyes is the director of the creative writing program at the University of Idaho and lives in Moscow, Idaho. She has published widely and several of her poems have been anthologized in *Eight Idaho Poets.* Some of her more recent work can be found in *Idaho's Poetry: A Centennial Anthology* (University of Idaho Press, Moscow, 1988) of which Ron McFarland is the editor.

Joan Fox was born in San Francisco in 1961. She earned a B.A. in English Literature from the University of California at Berkeley in 1985. Subsequently, she studied poetry and fiction writing with Alex Kuo at Washington State University and is presently working on her M.F.A. in Creative Writing at the University of Montana in Missoula.

Philip Garrison teaches English at Central Washington University in Ellensburg, Washington. He also spends much of his time in the deserts, mountains, and along the coastlines of Mexico. His poems, essays, and translations have appeared in numerous periodicals in this country and in Latin America. His collections of poetry include *A Woman and Certain Women, Lipstick* and *Away Awhile.*

Lynne Haley Slaughter has lived in Spokane for 10 years, where she earned a B.A. from Gonzaga University and an M.F.A. from Eastern Washington University. She has since performed duties as the publisher of *The Craft Network* and is the mother of two children, Cleo, 3, and baby Niles.

Mark Halperin teaches English at Central Washington University in Ellensburg, Washington and lives in "Clark's Flat" with his wife, the painter Barbara Scott, and their son, Noah. Trained in physics and pharmacology, he worked his way through the Writer's Workshop at the University of Iowa. His poems have been published in many magazines. He is the author of five books: *Backroads, The Whitecoverlet, Gomer,* and *A Place Made Fast.* His most recent book, *The Measure of Islands,* was published in 1990 by Wesleyan University Press.

Wes Hanson lives in Coeur d'Alene, Idaho and teaches English at Rathdrum High School, Idaho. He has won several awards for teaching excellence and was a Master teacher in the Whittenberger Project in English. A contributing poet at the Breadloaf Writer's Conference, he is also an accomplished watercolorist. His most recent exhibits were at "The Gallery" and at "Meckel Engineering," both in Coeur d'Alene.

James R. Hepworth teaches at Lewis-Clark State College in Lewiston, Idaho, where he is also the publisher of Confluence Press. His publications include *Silence as a Method of Birthcontrol* (poetry), *A Student's Guide to Freshman Composition* (text), and *Resist Much, Obey Little* (criticism, co-edited with Greg McNamee). His poems, interviews, reviews, and articles have appeared in various magazines, including *Western American Literature, The Bloomsbury Review,* and *The Paris Review.* Under his direction, Confluence Press has received three Western States Book Awards and a Pacific Northwest Bookseller's Award.

Christopher Howell has taught in writing programs throughout the West, most recently at Whitman College, Walla Walla, Washington. His poems have appeared in numerous periodicals, including *The Northwest Review, Ironwood, The Iowa Review, Hudson Review, North American Review,* and *Poetry Northwest. Sea Change* (L'Epervier), his fourth book of poems, won the King County Arts Commission's Book Project Award. Since 1972 he has been poetry editor for Lynx House Press and lives in Emporia, Kansas, where he teaches at Emporia State University.

Marc Hudson lived in Nespelem, Washington, where he was senior editor of the Chief Joseph Dam Archeology Project. Now residing in Greenbay, Wisconsin, he is the author of the 1977 chapbook, *Island*, and has contributed to *Poetry, New England Review, Malahat Review, Poetry Northwest, Willow Springs, Poetry Seattle, Breadloaf Quarterly, Prairie Schooner*, and *Sewanee Review*. He won the 1983 Juniper Prize, the annual poetry award sponsored by the University of Massachusetts Press, for *Afterlight*.

Christiane Jacox Kyle lives in Spokane, Washington and is program manager at Eastern Washington University's Women's Center. She also teaches English and Women's Studies after having taught on the Cheyenne Reservation in Montana, in the Montana Poets-in-the-Schools Program, and at Gonzaga University in Spokane. She received her M.F.A. in 1983 from Eastern Washington University. Her poems and translations have appeared in magazines and anthologies. In 1990 she received the Young Writers' Award from Yale University.

Eric Johnson was born in Salem, Oregon and lives in Pasco, Washington. He holds an M.F.A. degree from Eastern Washington University. Among his publications are "Walker," in *Ellipsis Magazine*; a translation of "The Wanderer," in *Willow Springs*; and the story, "The Haunted Horse," in *Frostfox Magazine*. He also has a science fiction novel that is looking for a publisher.

William Johnson teaches literature and writing at Lewis-Clark State College in Lewiston, Idaho. His poems have appeared in a variety of magazines and he has published scholarly work in the areas of medieval and American literature and linguistics. He enjoys family life and hiking and fishing in the Idaho backcountry.

Michael J. Kiefel, who lives in Spokane, Washington, has published numerous poems in college and small-press magazines. His chapbook, *The Daddy Ladder*, appeared in print in 1982. He has won several poetry awards, among them first place in the 1983 Dorothy Rosenberg Annual Poetry Awards. In 1985 he helped found "The Space Poets" community readings in Spokane. He has taught English locally at Gonzaga University, Heritage College, and Spokane Falls Community College.

Linda Kittell was born in 1952 in Troy, New York, but spent many summers on Lake Champlain listening to the Yankees on a little plastic radio. She received her B.A. in English and Greek from the University of Vermont and went on to the University of Montana for an M.F.A. in fiction and poetry. She lives now in Troy, Idaho and teaches composition and creative writing part-time at the University of Idaho and Washington State University.

Carolyn Kizer was born and raised in Spokane, Washington. Educated at Sarah Lawrence College, she was a Fellow of the Chinese Government in Comparative Literature at Columbia University, subsequently living in Nationalist China for a year. In 1964-65 she was a specialist in literature for the U.S. Department of State in Pakistan, and from 1966-1970 she served as the first director of the literature program of the National Endowment for the Arts. She has been Poet-in-Residence and Visiting Professor of Poetry at Columbia University, Stanford University, Princeton University, the University of Washington, Eastern Washington University, and many others. In 1959 she founded the poetry journal, *Poetry Northwest,* which she edited until 1965. The author of seven books of poetry and translations, the most recent one being *Carrying Over* (1988), she has received many awards, among them an Award from the American Academy and Institute of Arts and Letters, the Theodore Roethke Memorial Foundation Poetry Award, and the Pulitzer Prize for Poetry in 1985 for *Yin.*

Judith Kleck grew up on a ranch in the Southwest, but she has lived in the eastern Washington towns of Omak, Pullman, Toppenish and Ellensburg, where she currently teaches in the English Department at Central Washington University. She studied creative writing at the University of Arizona and has had poems published in *Poetry Northwest, Seattle Review, Southern Poetry Review* and other magazines.

Alex Kuo is the author of *The Window Tree, New Letters from Hiroshima and Other Poems,* and *Changing the River.* He lives in Moscow, Idaho and teaches creative writing at Washington State University, Pullman, Washington, where he is also the literary editor of the *Journal of Ethnic Studies.* His collection of short stories, *Between Lions,* was completed in Beijing, China, in the fall of 1989. He was awarded a National Endowment for the Arts Fiction Fellowship in 1990.

Laurie J. Lamon until recently lived in Spokane, Washington, where she taught in the English Department at Whitworth College. She received her B.A. in English from Whitworth in 1978; her M.F.A. in Creative Writing from the University of Montana in 1981; and her doctorate from the University of Utah. She resides in Seattle.

Eleanor Limmer lives with her husband and two children at Liberty Lake, Washington. She received a Master's Degree in Social Work from the University of Washington and is an accredited counselor and specialist in guided imagery and music for purposes of healing. She also is a freelance writer and works as the poetry editor of *Wildfire Magazine.*

James J. McAuley is Professor of English at Eastern Washington University, Cheney, Washington, where he also served as co-director of the creative writing program. He directs a summer writing workshop in Dublin each year and initiated the Brendan Behan Memorial Fellowship at Eastern Washington with the help of the Dublin City Council and the Arts Council of Ireland. The author of eight previous collections of poetry, a verse play (*The Revolution*), and a libretto (*Praise!*), he lives in Spokane, Washington. His latest book, *Coming and Going: New and Selected Poems,* was published in 1989 by the University of Arkansas Press.

Ron McFarland was born in Ohio, raised in Florida, taught in Texas two years, then earned his doctorate at the University of Illinois. Since 1970 he has taught at the University of Idaho, Moscow, Idaho, where he is Professor of English. He served as Idaho's first writer-in-residence. He is the author of a chapbook, *Certain Women*; a book of poems, *Composting at Forty*; a scholarly book, *The Villanelle: Evolution of a Poetic Form*; a textbook, *American Controversy*; four anthologies, *Eight Idaho Poets, James Welch, Norman Maclean*, and *The Idaho Poetry Anthology*; as well as a monograph, *David Wagoner*. Additional publications include over 150 poems, 50 scholarly articles, 27 essays, more than 20 short stories, and 15 reviews and notes.

James McKean taught literature and creative writing at Columbia Basin College, Pasco, Washington, for seventeen years. He was educated at Washington State College, where he was All-Coast (1967 and 68) in Basketball. Published in periodicals such as *Atlantic Monthly, Poetry, Northwest Review* and *Poetry Northwest*, he has held awards from the Seattle Arts Festival, the Great Lakes Colleges Association, and the Port Townsend Writers' Conference (Richard Hugo Memorial Fellowship). He has recently completed a Ph.D. in Literature at the University of Iowa, Iowa City, Iowa.

James R. McLeod lives in Coeur d'Alene, Idaho, where he is an English instructor and director of the Scottish Studies Program at North Idaho College. He has published widely on Theodore Roethke: *T.R.: A Bibliography; T. R.: A Manuscript Checklist; A Bibliographic Guide to Midwestern Literature*; and *Contemporary Authors: Bibliographic Series*. His poems have appeared in *Trestle Creek Review, Slackwater Review, Northwest Review* and other magazines. His most recent work is *Mysterious Lake Pend Oreille and Its "Monster."*

Fran Polek is Professor of English at Gonzaga University, specializing in American literature of the 20th century. He has also taught at the University of Missouri, the University of Southern California and the University of Arizona. He served as a Fulbright professor in Rumania for a year and received an award as Guest Scholar at the Smithsonian for continued work in Eastern European literature. His study of contemporary Rumanian poetry, "Red Stars and Eternity," was published in the *Journal of the Philological Association of the Pacific Coast*.

Joseph Powell teaches English at Central Washington University in Ellensburg, Washington. He received an M.F.A. from the University of Arizona in 1981. His first book, *Counting the Change*, was published in 1981 by *The Quarterly Review of Literature*; a second, called *Forgotten Fields*, is currently being circulated.

Steven Reames was educated at Whitworth College, Spokane, Washington, and Claremont Graduate School. He teaches English at Spokane Falls Community College. His family has lived in the Inland Empire for several generations, one branch in Potlatch, the other in Grant

County. "Making Idols" and "Biblical Ecology: A Second Look at the Garden of Eden" have recently been published by *Cross Currents*.

Franz Schneider is the translator (with Charles Gullans) of *Last Letters from Stalingrad* and the author of a collection of poems, *Roof of Stone*. Other work has appeared in *Hudson Review, Poetry Northwest, Poetry Seattle, Slackwater Review* and *Willow Springs*. He is currently Professor of English and Comparative Literature at Gonzaga University in Spokane, Washington.

Molly See lives near Leavenworth, Washington, and her work has appeared in publications throughout the West. She is a winner of the Bumbershoot Published Writer's Competition of the Seattle Arts Festival, and her book, *Sleeping Over*, was brought out in 1979 by Lynx House Press.

John P. Sisk is a widely published author whose work has appeared in *Atlantic Monthly, Harpers, The Hudson Review, Georgia Review, Salmagundi, Prairie Schooner* and many other periodicals and magazines. He is also the author of the book, *Persons and Institutions* and a winner of the Carl Foreman Award for his novel, *Trial of Strength*. A collection of his essays, *The Tyrannies of Virtue: The Cultural Criticism of John Sisk*, was recently published by Oklahoma University Press. After 50 years of teaching, he is now Professor Emeritus of English at Gonzaga University in Spokane, Washington.

Kornel Skovajsa received his Ph.D. in Comparative Literature from the University of Oregon. He teaches at Gonzaga University in Spokane, Washington, specializing in Modern British Literature and Literary Theory and Criticism. He has served as coordinator of Lower Division English, English Department Chair, Director of the Honors Program, and as a member of the Board of Regents. On the occasion of Gonzaga's centennial in 1987, he prepared for publication a special edition of the poetry of Gerard Manley Hopkins.

Ruth Slonim is Professor Emeritus of English at Washington State University. Author of four books of poetry, her poems and essays have been widely published in the U.S. and abroad. She has also held Invited Visiting Professorships at the University of Puerto Rico and the University of Dublin, Ireland. Her awards include the Governor's Arts Award and the Washington State University "Distinguished Faculty Address." She continues to make her home in Pullman, Washington.

Gerald E. Tiffany lives in Wenatchee, Washington, after ten years of residency in Spokane and a six year teaching stint at Spokane Community College. He has authored a chapbook, *Now Wind Takes the News*, and his poems and translations have appeared in *Prism International Anthology, New CollAge Magazine, Copula, Alaska Quarterly Review, The Forever Press*, and *Willow Springs*. He now teaches English at Wenatchee Valley College.

Patrick Todd lived nearly forty years in Montana but resides now in Spokane, Washington. He served three years as poet-in-residence for the State of Montana and directed the Poverello Center, a mission for transients and low income families, in Missoula from 1975-80. Married and the father of four children, Todd has earned two master's degrees and published three books of poetry. Presently, he teaches creative writing at Gonzaga University and Whitworth College in Spokane.

Georgia Toppe was born and raised in Spokane, Washington. After receiving her Performing Arts Degree and Master's in English from Indiana University, she taught piano and English in Indiana until returning to Spokane, where she has been an English teacher at Mead High School for the past four years. She has three children, Nicolle, Michele, and Mark.

Mary Ann Waters teaches writing and Spanish at West Valley High School in Spokane, Washington. In 1985 she co-authored a textbook, *Writing for Many Roles*, published by Boynton/Cook, and in 1987 her book of poems, *The Exact Place*, was published by Confluence Press of Lewiston, Idaho. She has held residencies at both the Yaddo and MacDowell colonies and in 1986 received a fellowship award from the Washington State Arts Commission.

Ronald Webster was born in 1939 in Okanogan, Washington, grew up in the Okanogan Valley, and worked in the valley apple orchards. He was educated at Gonzaga University in Spokane, Washington and has done graduate studies at Washington State University and at Texas A & M. His poems have appeared in *America, Western Poetry Quarterly, The Crab Creek Review,* and other small journals. He has lived in Canada and Peru. Currently, he lives near Colville in Stevens County where he works in the timber industry.

Mildred Weston was born in Waterville, Washington and has lived in Spokane since early childhood. She taught English Literature at Fort Wright College of the Holy Names for many years. Her poems appeared in such publications as *Poetry Northwest, Prairie Schooner, The Minnesota Review, The Northwest Review,* and the *New York Times.* Her books, *Vachel Lindsay: Poet in Exile* and *The Green Dusk: Selected Poems,* were published in 1987.

John Neal Williams grew up in Cedar Rapids, Iowa and was educated at Mankato State University and Washington State University. For the past ten years he has lived in the Palouse country near Colfax, Washington, where he teaches and is active in 4-H and youth soccer programs. Some of his work has appeared in *Windrow, MSU Today* and the *Spokane Chronicle.* In 1987 he won the Jerard *Windrow* Award as the outstanding non-fiction writer.

Fay Wright was born in Montana, grew up in the Puget Sound area, and now lives in Coeur d'Alene where she teaches writing and literature at North Idaho College. She has numerous publications to her credit and was a poetry editor of *Slackwater Review*. She is also the author of *Out of Season*, a book of poetry published by Confluence Press.

Robert Wrigley, an Illinois native, is Professor of English and Poet-in-Residence at Lewis-Clark State College in Lewiston, Idaho. He is widely published. Some of his poems have been reprinted in the *Anthology of Magazine Verse & Yearbook of American Poetry*. His books include, *The Sinking of Clay City*, *The Glow*, and *Moon in a Mason Jar*. He also is the recipient of two fellowships in poetry from the National Endowment for the Arts and the winner of the Poetry Society of America's 1985 Celia B. Wagner Award.